SPITFIRE HUNTERS

© 2010 Simon Parry

Design by Mark Postlethwaite
www.posart.com

Printed by
Melita Press
Malta

ISBN 978-0-95554735-5-5

First published 2010 by
Red Kite
PO Box 223,
Walton on Thames
Surrey, KT12 3YQ

Order this and similar publications directly from the publishers at great discounts.
www.redkitebooks.co.uk

Or simply scan the QR code above using your mobile phone for full details of all the special
discounts, along with more behind-the-scenes stories from the digs covered in this book.

SPITFIRE HUNTERS

by

Simon W Parry

CONTENTS

**Peter Foote (right) exhuming a Battle of Britain aircraft in 1965
just 25 years after the battle was fought.**

INTRODUCTION

Quite when or who dug up the first crashed aircraft in the name of archaeology is lost in the mists of time, but the late Peter Foote is a likely contender. Peter was one of the many war-time schoolboys who collected shrapnel and bomb splinters, or even parts of crashed planes. Unlike the majority of boys, however, Peter kept meticulous notes of war-time events. On one occasion he cycled from Bournemouth to Wareham to visit a Spitfire crash site and tried to fish out some wreckage with a grappling hook, but lost the hook; Sixty years later he retrieved his grappling hook when the Spitfire was excavated!

Of course the wreckage of most crashed aircraft was cleared superficially at the time. But there was a war on! Time and resources were dedicated to recovering the bodies of airmen killed in wrecks and, although scrap was valuable, there was no time and no equipment to salvage deeply buried wreckage.

Records detailing the location of wrecked aircraft during World War Two were at best perfunctory. Even in the UK there was no single 'list' of aircraft losses complied, in occupied Europe hardly any records survive. It was sufficient to know roughly where something was so that a salvage team could find the nearest village and ask the local constable. Seventy years later it is different matter, very few people remain who can recall the events of the war so clearly as to pin-point where an aircraft fell. The work of many over recent years has led to the recording of a huge volume of data for the first time, and before it is lost forever with the passing of the last eyewitnesses.

Archaeology

Noun

archaeology or archeology (är k - l -j)

The study of past human life and culture by the examination of physical remains.
[Greek arkhaiologia study of what is ancient]

Archaeology implies 'learning' from artifacts, so can anything truly be learned from recovering a 70 year-old-wreck?

Surprisingly, yes. Whilst the 'big picture' of World War Two and its aerial combats are well recorded, the minutiae of the events and machines have often been lost. Is it important to record where an incident happened, to identify the names of people involved? Who cares? Well, history does care.

Very few investigations made by people researching the air war in their area result in an excavation. The majority of incidents have left little or no physical trace and it is the rare occasion when something significant and tangible can be found that sparks people's interest. Occasionally an excavation has been seen as so significant that it has been the focus of a television documentary; these are the stories behind some of those excavations.

THE FIRST BLITZ

BBC TIMEWATCH

FIRST SHOWN 2006

DIRECTOR: JAMES HAYES-FISHER

PRODUCED BY: BBC HISTORY

THE FIRST BLITZ

On January 19th 1915 one of the technological marvels of the age made its appearance in the skies over Britain; Count von Zeppelin's airship. Only a decade before, man had taken his first tentative steps in to the air with powered machines, the Wright Brothers' small aeroplane and Zeppelin's giant gas bag. Now, just months into the Great War a new terror was to be unleashed on the world. Two Zeppelins had crossed the North Sea to the Norfolk coast and their crews had sent 24 bombs whistling down onto the towns below. Enormous for their time, the bombs weighed 50 kilos each and fell in the area from Great Yarmouth to Kings Lynn. Four people were killed and sixteen more injured. The nation was shocked. It was an outrage.

19 more raids were made on Britain during 1915, the 37 tons of bombs killed 181 people. Britain was defenceless. Searchlights roamed the skies, guns fired into the night and an occasional intrepid pilot ventured into the air in an attempt to bring a giant to earth, but to no effect. The Zeppelins were flying too high and too fast.

In July 1916 the Kaiser authorised raids on London and major towns – the age of indiscriminate bombing had begun. In 1916 125 tons of bombs were dropped in 23 raids. 293 people were killed. Still there was no effective

An early Zeppelin design

counter to the 'Baby Killers'. Finally, on September 2nd 1916, Lieutenant William Leefe Robinson succeeded in shooting down one of the sixteen raiders over London. The SL11 was not a true Zeppelin, rather a Schütte-Lanz machine with a wooden structure - not aluminium, but Leefe Robinson showed that the raiders were not invincible.

In the coming months improved British fighter aircraft and new incendiary ammunition turned the tide. The Germans had to improve their Zeppelins if they were to continue raiding England.

Postcards depicting the destruction of the 'Zepps' were very popular and sold widely. Often a local printer would add the name of his home town to the cards to add a local flavour to help sales.

THE END OF THE "BABY-KILLER."

ZEPP WRECKAGE.   SERIES. A
CROWN COPYRIGHT RES.

Hero of the moment, Lieutenant William Leefe Robinson, who shot down
SL11 on September 2nd 1916, and right one of the many postcards
published to commemorate the deed.

In March 1917 the latest Zeppelins arrived over Britain. Stripped of all comforts, streamlined and lighter, the new 'height climbers' cruised at over 65 mph and could climb to over 3 ½ miles high. The Zeppelin crewmen were now flying higher and for longer than man had ever done. The forces and effects of altitude were barely understood. Wind speeds were far higher than at ground level and temperatures plummeted to those at the arctic. Equipment regularly failed and men suffered from lack of oxygen that befuddled their minds and frostbite that numbed their hands.

The 'height climber' L48 was the ninety-fifth Zeppelin built and was also known as LZ95 (Luftschiff Zeppelin 95) it was the German Navy's forty-eighth 'Luftschiff' and so became the L48. She made her maiden flight on 22nd May 1917 still under manufacturer's hands (as LZ95) and her first raid on Britain (as L48) on 17th June 1917. Her first raid was destined to be her last.

"SPOTTED."
THE ZEPP RAIDER.
Passed for publication, by Press Bureau.

In the early hours L48 crossed the east coast of England and headed for the port of Harwich. Technical problems had already manifested themselves, one engine had failed and another was beginning to fail. The navigational compass had frozen and the captain decided to release his bombs and make a quick getaway while he could. As the bombs exploded harmlessly in the fields below, the searchlights and gun batteries latched onto the Zeppelin. The searchlight beams illuminated the huge Zeppelin and artillery shells exploded around it. Four fighter pilots from the Royal Flying Corps were already in pursuit. Frank Holder and his gunner in an FE2b found L48 bracketed by lights and gunfire, but the ungainly pusher biplane could not climb high enough. Kapitänleutnant Eichler gave his orders to head east across the North Sea and come down a mile in height to 13,000 feet. Mislead by the frozen compass the navigator headed north, over the Suffolk coast. Then a second engined failed and the airspeed dropped still further.

A radio message from headquarters suggested that L48 come down still further to 11,000 feet where westerly winds would speed them back. Doggedly, Holder had kept up his pursuit and L48 was now coming down to him. Sydney Ashby, Holder's gunner, emptied drum after drum of ammunition at the Zeppelin, but to no effect. Then the gun jammed. Previously they had seen their sparking, fizzling, tracers whiz away through the dark night sky, like thousands of cigarette ends all flicked at the same time, streaking away before being frustratingly absorbed into the giant shape of the invader. Then two more fighter aircraft joined the fray. Henry Saundby was there in a DH2 and Don Watkins joined them in a BE12. The three fragile stick-and-string biplanes flew after the giant Zeppelin like moths to a flame. The Zeppelin was 645 feet long and the fighter pilots closed to just 150 feet – they were like rowing boats assaulting a battleship. Setting fire to a Zeppelin was no easy task for the gas bags had first to be punctured and the hydrogen ignited when mixed with air, but a recently designed incendiary bullet made all the difference – L48 was alight!

The initial glow grew rapidly into an all consuming inferno in seconds and lit up both the sky and the ground below in an eerie light. Thousand of onlookers cheered and stared, mesmerised at the spectacle.

Next the Zeppelin broke its back amidships and began its final plunge to earth. With both bow and stern pointing skywards it assumed the form of a V-shape, wreathed in flames that towered several hundreds of feet into the air. Explosions rent the air as the last gas bags exploded.

Trapped in the control and engine gondolas the crew had no means of escape from the flames that raged above them. The heavy fur coats, gloves and hats that insulated them from the intense cold now served to protect them from the heat of the flames as they cowered on the deck. Their agony lasted over three minutes as the airborne inferno tumbled the two miles to earth.

THE STRAFED ZEPP. L48. June 17, 1917. No. 6   J. S. Waddell, Photo. Leiston

People were drawn to the funeral pyre from miles around. An horrific sight greeted the first to arrive who risked their own lives to search for survivors. Otto Mieth was pulled alive for under the burnt bodies of his comrades who had collapsed on top of him. Heinrich Ellerkamm rode the wreck to the ground, clinging to girders until the ship hit the ground. Winded but conscious he forced his way through the hot girders and blazing fuel to the field beyond where he was found wandering in a daze. Wilhelm Uecker was rescued from an engine gondola by locals. Six men had chosen to jump from the control gondola and were found dead in a nearby field, one buried up to his knees after landing feet-first. Ten others were burnt alive.

THE STRAFED ZEPP. L48, June 17, 1917.   No. 17   J. S. Waddell, Photo. Leiston

Local photographer J S Waddell of Leiston did a roaring trade in photographic postcards of L48's wreckage.

The "Strafed" Zepp.   3·45 a.m., 17th June, 1917.   No. 4.   Published by J. S. Waddell, Photographer, Leiston

THE LAST FLIGHT OF THE L48

0   2   4   6   8   10 miles

03.30hrs L48 crashes at Theberton

03.25hrs Saundby, Holder and Watkins all attack

02.17hrs L48 at 18,400ft

03.15hrs L48 at 12,000ft and in difficulties

03.10hrs Saundby opens fire

LEISTON

ALDEBURGH

Two engines fail L48 drops to 11,000ft

01.50hrs Clarke takes off in a BE2C
01.55hrs Holder takes off in an FeE2b
02.55hrs Saundby takes off ia a DH2

WOODBRIDGE

ORFORD

L48 at 13,000ft

L48 inbound at 17,000ft

01.45hrs L48 stops for 15 minutes to repair engines

IPSWICH

02.45hrs Bombs dropped on Falkenham and Kirton

FELIXSTOWE

HARWICH

02.30hrs Harwich guns open fire

Strong south-westerly winds

02.00hrs Watkins takes off from Goldhangar in a BE12

The authorities arrived at Holly Tree Farm, and took charge of the wreck. The area was cordoned off as intelligence officers immediately began to inspect the remains. Of great interest was a set of German naval radio codes discovered in the charred control gondola. The structure itself was significant for this was the first 'height climber' to fall into British hands. The salvage operation was conducted by the Admiralty's Constructional Department that oversaw the dismantling of the Zeppelin. Visitors were allowed into the field for a small fee and were kept behind the cordoned off area. A stream of lorries transported the parts to Leiston railway station until the only thing marking the spot where L48 had fallen was a burnt area of earth.

Another souvenir postcard showing the mountain of German metal piled high in a quiet Norfolk field.

ZEPPELIN ARCHAEOLOGY

Dr Neil Faulkner and his Great War Archaeology Group (GWAG) had been working with John Farren, commissioning editor for BBC2's Timewatch, on a project that became known as 'The First Blitz'. Although regular excavations are now carried out in France and Belgium on the battlefields of the First World War, no one had applied archaeological methods to the home defences. The airfields at North Weald Bassett and Chingford were examined as were anti aircraft gun positions at Waltham Abbey and Southwark, but was anything left of the raiders themselves?

Well known metal detector user and GWAG contributor Julian Evan-Hart was brought in to assess the possibility of there being anything at all left at any of the five Zeppelin crash sites in Britain. The site where SL11 fell at Cuffley is now covered by a housing estate, as is the place where L31 came down. It was soon established that only at L48's site was there any real chance of anything meaningful being found. The site at Croft's Field, on what has been re-named Theberton Hall Farm, was searched in April 2006 and the results seemed to be encouraging. An assortment of small finds led to the tempting possibility that there could be something buried at the points where the huge Maybach engines had hit the ground. Photographs seemed to support the idea that the engines had been ripped from the gondolas and crashed to the ground. A full-scale dig was organised by the GWAG for June 2006, to be filmed under the direction of John Hayes-Fisher for the planned Timewatch programme.

Neil Faulkner and the GWAG were excited at the prospect of the excavation. No one had attempted to excavate a

Dr Neil Faulkner and his Great War Archaeology Group (GWAG) apply traditional archaeological methods to the L48 crash site.

Zeppelin site before, this was breaking new ground, but would anything be found of a lighter-than-air ship 90 years after its crash?

In the couple of months since the initial site visit the crop of barley had grown significantly and the area assumed to have been the main impact point lay somewhere in the middle of it. A key location feature in aerial photos of the crash was a hedge line that once ran across the field, but that had been removed many decades ago. Fortunately the keen eye of the archaeologist came to the rescue and identified a strip of barley that had grown better than the rest of field – a miniature crop-mark to show where the hedge and ditch had once been. About halfway along the old hedge the metal detectors re-located the impact point and some tiny fragments of L48. Although there was no doubt that endless fragments would be found in the plough soil, everyone wanted to know what lay below this.

A digger was brought in to scrape away the soil down to plough depth and the resulting spoil heap was searched by detectors. Contemporary reports suggested that at least one of the engines had been torn from its mounting and partially buried itself in the ground. It had been hoped that it would be possible to identify the resulting hole from soil disturbance and discolouration from oil and fuel, there might even be some engine parts left in the ground. The entire area of the field that had once been covered was excavated to below plough depth. The site was 'Geofizzed', GPS'd, dug, scraped,

Julian Evan-Hart explains the button's significance to director John Hayes-Fisher and his crew. (David Stuckey)

detected, probed and prodded, but no trace of an impact point could be located. L48 had weighed 25 tons and had fallen two miles to the ground, surely something would have pushed itself more than one foot into the soft soil? At length it was reasoned that the structure, remaining gas bags and the remnants of the outer covering had acted a parachute and slowed the decent to 60 or 70 miles an hour, perhaps even less. After the stern had hit the ground the main structure slowly collapsed and acted as a 'shock absorber'. The resulting impact had, after all, been survivable for three men.

WHO SHOT DOWN THE L48?

L48 had approached the English coast at a height of 13,000 feet; she was part of a force of four airships sent to attack London. L48 drifted over Orfordness at about 02.00 hours. From here she rounded Wickham Market. Bombs were dropped around Harwich with one being dropped over Martlesham. Once the bombs had been released the ship headed north

The German Naval Officer's button discovered at the site. Not the largest of finds, but a poignant one.

along the coast. At this point anti aircraft guns opened up both from coastal batteries and from several on ships out at sea. Searchlights flicked on and wavered about the sky finally focusing on the L48, seemingly supporting her on their beams in the night sky. A number of pilots spotted her pinpointed by searchlights and bursts of AA fire. Flying a BE2c (A8896) from the Armament Experimental Station at Orfordness, Lt EW Clarke was the first to attack. Between Orfordness and Harwich he fired a total of four drums of Lewis gun ammunition from 11,000 feet at the airship which was still 2,000 feet higher. However there seemed to be no effect at all for this expenditure of ammunition. The second aeroplane to attack was an FE2b B401 crewed by Lt FD Holder (Pilot) and Sgt S Ashby also from the AES, this crew also fired four drums of Lewis ammunition, and an additional thirty rounds from a fifth drum when suddenly their gun jammed. As this happened they were approximately five miles from Leiston and frustratingly within 300 yards range of their target. Captain R H M S Saundby in DH2 A5058 managed to fire two and a half drums at the target.* The airship was finally chased by Lt P Watkins in BE12 6610 from 37 (HD) Sqn (A Flight) at Goldhanger, he fired another two drums from 2,000 down to 1,000 feet, and then another from 500feet. It was Watkins who was officially credited with the final 'Kill' of L48.

All Pilots used standard 0.303 rounds of both ball and incendiary ammunition. The credit given to Watkins for shooting down L48 was purely arbitrary and probably the result of higher authority wanting such credit to go to the Home Defence organisation.

The crew of L48 who were killed were:-

Viktor Schutze, Korvettenkapitan,
Kommodore of the North Sea Airship Division.
Franz Georg Eichler *Kapitänleutnant*
Heinrich Ahrens
Wilhelm Betz
Walter Dippmann
Wilhelm Gluckel
Paul Hannemann
Heinrich Herbst
Franz Konig
Wilhelm Meyer
Karl Milich
Michael Neunzig
Karl Floger
Paul Suchlich
Herman Van Stockum
Paul Westphal.

*Saundby was later awarded the Military Cross for his part in this action and retired from the RAF in 1946 with the rank of Air Vice Marshal.

The largest part of L48 to turn up was this section of girder - not found on the site, but in an antique shop where it served as an umbrella stand.

The survivors were:-

Wilhelm Uecker
Otto Miethe
Heinrich Ellerkamm
(said to be wandering around dazed after the crash).

Note: - It is believed to be Ellerkamm who was the crew member taken to a local house in Theberton. When the door opened and the occupant asked if she could look after him until the arrival of the authorities, her reply was, "Not likely, lock the bugger in the shed."

The Zeppelin War
Zeppelins built in WW1 - 84
Zeppelins lost in WW1 – 60
Raids on Britain - 51
Bombs dropped - 5,806
Casualties:
Killed 557
Injured 1,358
Britain's Zeppelin defence tied-up
12 fighter squadrons and over 10,000 men.

As if a reminder of the loss of life in this tranquil field, poppies grew there as the excavation progressed.
(Dr Nadia Durrani, from 'In Search of the Zeppelin War – The Archaeology of the First Blitz').

BILLY DRAKE AND THE FIGHTER BOYS

BBC2

FIRST SHOWN 2004

PRODUCER / DIRECTOR

JOHN HAYES-FISHER

PRODUCED BY BBC HISTORY

BILLY DRAKE AND THE FIGHTER BOYS

"I am speaking to you from the Cabinet Room at 10 Downing Street. This morning, the British Ambassador in Berlin handed the German government a final note, stating that unless we heard from them by 11 o'clock that they were prepared at once to withdraw their troops from Poland, a state of war would exist between us. I have to tell you now that no such undertaking has been received, and that consequently this country is at war with Germany.

"The situation in which no word given by Germany's ruler could be trusted and no people or country could feel itself safe, has become intolerable. And now we have resolved to finish it, I know that you will all play your part.

"May God bless you all. And may He defend the right, for it is evil things that we shall be fighting against – brute force, bad faith, injustice, oppression and persecution; and against them I am certain that right will prevail."

Prime Minister Neville Chamberlain
11.15 a.m. 3rd Sept. 1939

A 73 Squadron Hurricane of the AASF during the 'Phoney War'.

AASF Hurricanes pose for an RAF photographer over France on 19th April 1940. The photo was taken from the rear cockpit of a Fairey Battle.

Just five days after Chamberlain's speech, fifteen Hurricanes of No.1 Squadron left Tangmere for France to become part of the Advanced Air Striking Force. The AASF had ten squadrons of Fairey Battle light bombers and two squadrons of Hurricanes, Nos.1 and 73. The pilots braced themselves to repulse the German invasion, but none came.

It was on October 30th 1939 that a pilot from No.1 Squadron created a small piece of history; Pilot Officer 'Boy' Mould shot down a Luftwaffe reconnaissance Dornier 17, the first RAF fighter victory in France during World War Two. The months of waiting continued through the bleak winter of 1939/40 into spring, a period christened the 'phoney war'. As the weather improved so the Luftwaffe activity increased until by the end of April the pilots of No.1 Squadron had claimed 23 victories, for the loss of five Hurricanes and one pilot killed. But something was brewing over the border.

On 10th May 1940, the Germans struck. The Blitzkrieg tactics used so successfully against Poland the year before were turned on France, Holland and Belgium. Wehrmacht paratroopers landed and tanks and infantry followed the Luftwaffe bombers.

The pilots of No.1 Squadron went into action and, by 13th May, had claimed 40 German aircraft shot down, for the loss of nine Hurricanes. The Squadron had been heavily engaged on May 13th. One pilot, Pilot Officer Billy Drake, had been attacked by a Messerschmitt Bf 110, and managed to bale out of his burning Hurricane, but he had been seriously injured. Billy was in a flight of six Hurricanes led by Flight Lieutenant Prosser Hanks, but he was having trouble with his oxygen system and was forced to leave his section and head back to his airfield at Berry-au-Bac. He recalled:

"On the way back I saw three Dorniers. I shot down the one on the left. I switched over from the left-hand side of the formation and as I was lining up to shoot there was a big thump. A German had got behind me and I never saw him at all. He got me really good and proper because I was in flames straight away. I must have been at about 12,000 feet."

The combined machinegun and cannon fire from an Me110 had punctured the fuel tank that was situated immediately in front of the cockpit and petrol had sprayed into the cockpit, soaking Billy's clothes.

"I felt that I had been wounded in the legs and back, but I had no idea if it was serious or not. So I did everything necessary to bale out; undoing the Sutton Harness that keeps the pilot in his seat, and then I tried to get out, but I had forgotten to open the hood, which probably saved my life because the flames were coming up and I was covered in petrol! Had I opened the hood the flames would have come into the cockpit and probably burnt me very badly or even killed me. By the time I realised what I hadn't done I turned on my back, opened the hood and fell out.

"When I opened my parachute I heard the roar of engines and the noise of machineguns and saw tracer bullets passing all round me. The Messerschmitt had followed me down and was trying to shoot me up as I dangled on the end of my parachute. I tried to spill air out of my parachute to increase the rate of descent and so avoid the bullets, but I found I couldn't raise my right arm because of the wounds in my back. But eventually the Messerschmitt joined his formation and left me to float gently to the ground – luckily not having hit me."

Several townsfolk had seen the combat and followed Billy's parachute to the ground. They picked him up and took him to a hospital at Rethel.

Billy Drake was shot down by an Me110 similar to this one. The twin engined German fighter was slower than a Hurricane but had a far more powerful armament.

GROUP CAPTAIN BILLY DRAKE DSO DFC*

Billy Drake was a Londoner, born in 1917. He joined the RAF in 1936 and on completion of his training was posted to No.1 Squadron in 1937. The first enemy aircraft he brought down was an Me109 on 20th April, 1940. When the invasion came on 10th May he shot down an He111 and on 13th May a Dornier 17, but he was then shot down by Me110s. Like several of his fellow pilots Billy was sent to a training unit to pass on his hard-earned skills to new pilots entering the Battle of Britain. Back on operations he became a flight commander, then went back to an OTU and was then posted to West Africa to command his own squadron. Moving to the Middle East in 1942 he began to increase his total of enemy aircraft destroyed before a series of staff posts. He retired from the RAF in 1963 as a Group Captain.

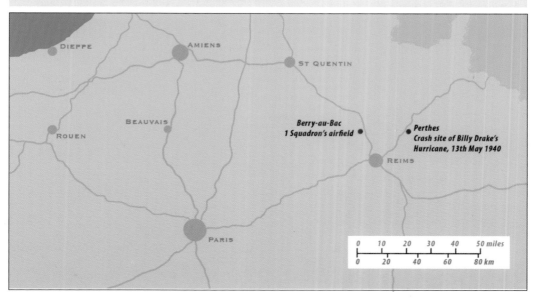

63 YEARS ON

Documentary maker John Hayes-Fisher developed an interest in the exploits of No.1 Squadron during the Battle of France and proposed the idea to the BBC. Key to the plan was Billy Drake, a sprightly 86 year-old in 2003. John was also fascinated by the idea of tracing the Hurricane that Billy had baled out of 63 years before and the effort to locate the wreck would be an important element in the documentary. Veteran aviation archaeologist Steve Vizard had already traced the Hurricane of Billy's fellow squadron member Paul Richey, author of the classic war-time book 'Fighter Pilot'; could he also find Billy Drake's machine? It was recorded that Billy had been brought down near Perthes and local researcher Jean-Michel Goyat had an idea of where it might have fallen, but actually finding the site was still down to hours of field work. Long before the cameras appeared the first tell-tale remains surfaced, brackets from the Hurricane's structure and a few rounds of exploded 303 ammunition. The ground at the crash site on a hillside at le fond de Norglette was very hard. The top soil was only half a metre deep and then it became solid chalk; would anything of significance still be buried?

Steve Vizard with the oxygen bottle that had forced Billy to leave his squadron, and Billy himself in the blue jacket.

Billy is given permission to find his old Hurricane by the Mayor of Perthes.

To excavate the wreck of an aircraft in France several permissions must be sought, notably that of the town's Mayor. In a touching and light-hearted ceremony the Mayor of Perthes granted Billy permission to excavate his own aircraft!

In September 2003 the excavation began but, as predicted, the rock-hard ground had taken its toll. Not only had the Hurricane broken up, but the action of water and air had caused the little remaining to corrode badly.

Although only shattered fragments of the Hurricane were found, several pieces key to the story were discovered. The oxygen bottle that had not been re-filled and had caused Billy to turn back; the gun sight he had last seen the Dorniers through; the Browning guns and, most importantly, the piece of steel armour that had protected his head.

Today it is taken for granted that the aircraft of the RAF in World War Two had some form of armour protection for the pilot, but this was not always the case. In the inter-war years performance of aircraft was the priority and any increase in weight would compromise that; big sheets of steel to protect the pilot were not

wanted. At the outbreak of war neither the Hurricane or Spitfire carried armour behind the pilot; one Staff Officer even wrote that only a fool would allow himself to be shot at from behind! An incident involving No.1 Squadron was instrumental in changing this. In November 1939 Flying Officer 'Pussy' Palmer was leading a Section from 'A' Flight when he attacked a Dornier 17 bomber that had one engine on fire and from which the rear gunner and the navigator had already baled out. The Dornier's pilot suddenly throttled back, slipped onto Palmer's tail and put 'exactly 34' bullets through his Hurricane. One of the bullets penetrated

Above: A small but vital piece of wreckage bearing the Hurricane's previously unknown serial number P2695.

Below: A close up of the all important armour plate that was installed behind the pilot's head following No. 1 Squadron's experiences in France.

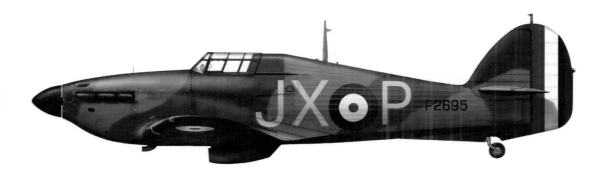

A profile of Billy Drake's Hurricane as it would have looked in early 1940. Some days before it was shot down, orders had been sent to all squadrons to add a yellow outer to the fuselage roundel and apply the fin flash to the tail and not the rudder, it is not known whether these alterations were applied to this aircraft. Both 1 and 73 Squadron also removed their squadron code letters for a time whilst in France which again may have applied to this aircraft.

86 year old Billy Drake is re-introduced to the piece of armour plate that saved his life back in May 1940 by historian Peter Arnold.

the locker behind Palmer's head and smashed the windscreen.

Paul Richey described the subsequent events in his book 'Fighter Pilot':

"Pussy's combat had an important sequel that was to save the lives of many RAF pilots. At this time the only armour our fighters carried was a thick cowling over the front petrol tank and a bullet-proof windscreen, while the Battles had thick armour behind the pilot - as indeed did the German fighters. After Pussy's lucky escape [he had crashed without injury after the incident] we decided we should have back armour too, and we asked for it. ...the Air Ministry refused our request because the experts maintained that back armour would affect the Hurricane's centre of gravity and lead to flying difficulties."

Squadron Leader Bull Halahan, Commanding Officer of No.1 Squadron, ordered that back armour from a Fairey Battle be fitted into a Hurricane and then carried out the flying tests himself.

Whether as a result of Squadron Leader Halahan's initiative or coincidentally, No.1 Squadron was soon equipped with Hurricanes fitted with rear armour. Soon enough, at any rate, for Billy Drake. Gunfire from the Me110 struck his Hurricane from behind, but Billy still received wounds in his back and legs from shell splinters and bullets that entered through the hole made for his seat harness straps in his rear armour plate and through other unprotected areas.

Once cleaned, the head armour found at the crash site showed a near penetration by a bullet that would, to Billy Drake's mind, have been the end of him had the armour been less able to resist the impact - or, of course, had it not been there at all!

Billy, with the piece of steel that had saved his life 63 years before.

DUNKIRK SPITFIRE

SPITFIRE MK.I P9373 92 (EAST INDIA) SQUADRON
SERGEANT PAUL KLIPSCH

23 MAY 1940   -   WIERRE-EFFROY

TIME TEAM

CHANNEL 4

FIRST SHOWN JANUARY 2000

PRODUCER / DIRECTOR: JEREMY CROSS

THE DUNKIRK SPITFIRE

    "I would remind the Air Council that the last estimate which they made as to the force necessary to defend this country was fifty-two squadrons, and my strength has now been reduced to the equivalent of thirty-six squadrons.

    "I must therefore request that as a matter of paramount urgency the Air Ministry will consider and decide what level of strength is to be left to the Fighter Command for the defence of this country, and will assure me that when the level has been reached, not one fighter will be sent across the Channel however urgent and insistent the appeals for help may be.

    "I believe that if an adequate fighter force is kept in this country, if the Fleet remains in being, and if Home Forces are suitably organized to resist invasion, we should be able to carry on the war single-handed for some time, if not indefinitely. But, if the Home Defence Force is drained away in desperate attempts to remedy the situation in France, defeat in France will involve the final, complete and irremediable defeat of this country."

H. C. T. Dowding
Air Chief Marshal
Letter to the Air Ministry. 16th May 1940

And so the line was drawn that no further air support should be sent to France. In less than two weeks the German Blitzkrieg had taken most of Europe and on May 23rd was poised to push the forces trapped in the Dunkirk pocket into the sea. It was now important to save as many men as possible from France and to that end Dowding was obliged to send fighters based in England over the Channel to hinder the Luftwaffe in its attacks on the troops attempting to evacuate.

On the morning of May 23rd the German 2nd Panzer Division began its attack on Boulogne and for the first time Spitfires were thrown into the fray in numbers. One of the Spitfire squadrons making its debut was No.92 Squadron, based at Northolt. The entry of that day in the Operational Record Book – Form 540 reads:

"The whole squadron left at dawn for Hornchurch where they commenced patrol flying over the French coast. At about 08.30 hours they ran into 6 Messerschmitts and a dog-fight ensued. The result was a great victory for 92 Squadron and all 6 German machines (Me109s) were brought down with only one loss to us. It is with greatest regret that we lost Pilot Officer P. A. G. Learmond in this fight. He was seen to come down in flames over Dunkerque.

"In the afternoon the squadron went out again on patrol and this time encountered at least 40 Messerschmitts flying in close formation. The result of this fight was another 17 German machines (Me110s) were brought down and 92 Squadron lost Squadron Leader R. J. Bushell – the Commanding Officer – Flying Officer J. Gillies and Sergeant P Klipsch (566457). Flight Lieutenant C. P. Green was wounded in the leg and is now in hospital at Shorncliffe. The remainder of the

A wrecked Spitfire lies in the sand as several did after the battles around Dunkirk.

squadron returned to Hornchurch badly 'shot up' with 7 Spitfires unserviceable. It has been a glorious day for the squadron, with 33 German machines brought down, but the loss of the Commanding Officer and the three others has been a very severe blow to us all, and to the squadron which was created and trained last October by our late Squadron Leader."

Roger Bushell and the Great Escape

Bushell had been the Squadron Leader much missed by the squadron as the diarist noted, but he had not been killed as the report suggests. He baled out successfully, but fell into German hands. Later his name came to the fore as leader of an escape from Stalag Luft III, immortalised in the book and film 'The Great Escape'. Bushell, played in the legendary film by Richard Attenborough, (as the character Bartlett), took part in several escape attempts and was warned that if he tried again he would be shot. Known as 'Big X' he organised the escape from the north camp at Stalag Luft III on 24-25 March 1944 when 76 men escaped; most were captured and 50, including Roger, were executed.

Wierre-Effroy is a village 12 kilometres north-east of Boulogne on the old N.1 road to Calais; for its people May 23rd 1940 was to be a significant day. They had been waiting anxiously for the Germans to come and their arrival appeared to have been heralded by an air battle fought overhead. An English plane had crashed in flames and within hours the German advance had pushed through village; they were now living under enemy occupation. In the days that followed the villagers took it upon themselves to recover the unfortunate pilot's body and bury it at their 16th Century church. Later the pilot was identified as Paul Henry Klipsch, a 24 year old Sergeant Pilot from Watford, Hertfordshire.

The British garrison in Boulogne surrendered on May 25th, but by that time 4,368 troops had been evacuated from the port. Operation Dynamo, the evacuation of Dunkirk, began the following day; eventually 218,226 British and 120,000 French troops were taken off the beaches.

Opposite page: Phil Harding and Mick Aston making the first finds on the site.

Spitfire Crash site 23rd May 1940
Wierre-Effroy

The crash site of Paul Klipsch's Spitfire was first located by the late Alan Brown and his wife. The pair spent their holidays touring Europe in their psychedelically painted VW camper van searching for aircraft wrecks. The presence of the grave in the church had prompted Alan to make enquiries as to the location of crash site and it had soon been pointed out to him. Not far below the surface he found the breech of a Browning machine-gun buried vertically in the clay; it seemed very likely that the aircraft had dived steeply into the ground and that a lot of it was still

there. Coincidentally, a TimeTeam researcher had approached Steve Vizard at that time with a proposal to feature a Spitfire recovery in a future programme. Steve thought that Alan's discovery might make a particularly interesting topic and the long road to making the idea a reality began.

After a year in the planning the excavation, organised by Jean-Michel Goyat, was carried out over the now famous 'just three days' in June 1999. The TimeTeam circus had rolled into town the previous day, complete with catering bus and toilets, and the 'incident room' had been established behind the café at the cross roads. Steve Vizard assembled a team of experts including Spitfire Guru Peter Arnold to assist and identify the parts recovered. The production company brought air accident investigator Steve Moss to establish the circumstances of the crash. The excavation itself would be conducted by the regular TimeTeam 'diggers' and was planned as a fusion of regular archaeology with aircraft archaeo-salvage. The previous aircraft excavation for TimeTeam, the Reedham Marsh B-17, had not gone well for the production team and all involved were concerned that there would be no repeat of the 'clash of cultures' that had been a feature of that dig.

Carenza Lewis and Mark Kirby work together excavating one of the machine-guns. One of the parts still had the Spitfire's serial number painted on it.

Although a huge hole was dug care was taken to find even the smallest fragments, like this section of the manufacturer's label, only 40 millimetres long.

Operations on the first day began with 'field walking' by eye, and later with detectors, to establish the extent of the debris. As soon as this began a remarkable thing happened; the aviation experts found only aircraft, but the archaeologists found only Roman pottery! Clearly each had an eye for their own particular finds. The location of the Browning found earlier by Alan Brown was carefully excavated by Carenza and Mark Kirby working in harmony. From this small square one of the more significant finds of the dig emerged, part of a gun ammunition feed with the Spitfire's serial number painted in it, proof that this was Paul Klipsch's machine. Part of the programme's brief had been fulfilled in the first day.

For the remainder of day one and day two the excavation, layer-by-layer, continued. The excavator was used only to clear the area around the wreck that began to tower from the bottom of the hole. At the top of the wreck was the tail wheel, still with its tyre attached. By the end of the second day progress had slowed as the diggers struggled with the sticky clay at the bottom of the pit. Conventional archaeological methods had gone as far as they could; digging with spade and trowel, while sitting in a puddle of high-octane petrol, was not an option. That evening Mick Worthington and a small team stayed with the excavator to dig down to the front of the engine - around ten feet down.

A unique event had been organised for the final day. Display pilot Charlie Brown had flown Guy Black's Mark V Spitfire BM597 to Calais airport where

It's not currently known what individual code letter Paul Klipsch's Spitfire carried but it would have looked very similar to Roger Bushell's Spitfire (above) shot down on the same day.

A full-sized plan of a Spitfire was cut from plastic sheets and used to position the parts as they were recovered. In September 2008 the airframe was put on the UK civil register of aircraft as G-CFGN and will, one day, be re-built.

Paul Klipsch's grave in the tiny churchyard at Wierre-Effroy.

Allan Wright would be filmed sitting in a Spitfire for the fist time since the war. Allan had flown in the same combat in which Paul Klipsch had been shot down. It also afforded Phil Harding a chance to display his metalwork skills as he was coached by an expert from Steve's company, Airframe Assemblies, in repairing part of a Spitfire. That afternoon Charlie flew BM597 to Wierre-Effroy for some low-level fly-pasts and a manoeuvre that those on the ground will remember for many-a-year. Charlie gained height and rolled the Spitfire over into a screaming dive, pulling-out just over the crash site and roared low overhead.

The remains of Paul Klipsch's Spitfire were finally lifted from the hole and the aviation team took over to disentangle the wreck and position the parts on a full size silhouette of a Spitfire that had been laid out on the ground. An estimated 50 to 60% of the airframe had been unearthed, mostly from the fuselage. Only some machine guns that had been torn out of their mountings and speared into the ground marked the position of the wings, the wings themselves having been left on the surface of the field.

The final act was for Guy and Tony Robinson to explain their findings to Paul's half-brother Eric Wynn-Owen. Behind-the-scenes research by John Foreman had identified the German unit that had engaged 92 Squadron and the pilot who had shot Paul Klipsch down. The Me110s had been from I Zerstörergeschwader (destroyer squadron) 26 and the victor was probably Gunther Specht, who was also shot down that day. Specht went on to become one of Germany's leading fighter

aces, but was killed in January 1945. The three days had proved to be an emotional and trying time for all involved, with moments of excitement and others of deep reflection. Eric Wynn-Owen had been clearly moved to finally discover what had befallen Paul and to visit the grave. Sadly Eric passed away before the programme was televised. With the excavation over, the wreckage was brought to England for further detailed examination. When the crushed map box was opened a map was found with Roger Bushell's signature on it. Several holes that may well have been caused by cannon or machine-gun fire were found in the airframe, but Steve Moss found a single hole of particular significance. A machine-gun calibre hole was identified in the cockpit side door, angled and in such a position that the bullet would likely have killed or incapacitated Paul Klipsch in the air.

FIGHTER DIG LIVE

CHANNEL 5

FIRST SHOWN 30 MAY 2004

DIRECTOR: EDWINA SILVER

PRODUCED BY: MENTORN

ALSO SHOWN AS:

SEARCH FOR THE LOST FIGHTER PLANE
NATIONAL GEOGRAPHIC CHANNEL

FIGHTER DIG LIVE

"What General Weygand called the Battle of France is over. I expect that the Battle of Britain is about to begin. Upon this battle depends the survival of Christian civilization. Upon it depends our own British life, and the long continuity of our institutions and our Empire. The whole fury and might of the enemy must very soon be turned on us. Hitler knows that he will have to break us in this Island or lose the war. If we can stand up to him, all Europe may be free and the life of the world may move forward into broad, sunlit uplands. But if we fail, then the whole world, including the United States, including all that we have known and cared for, will sink into the abyss of a new Dark Age made more sinister, and perhaps more protracted, by the lights of perverted science. Let us therefore brace ourselves to our duties, and so bear ourselves that, if the British Empire and its Commonwealth last for a thousand years, men will still say, 'This was their finest hour'."

So ended Winston Churchill's speech to the House of Commons on 18th June 1940. In a few weeks Hitler's 'Blitzkrieg' had rolled over western Europe and the might of the German military machine stood within sight of the last stronghold of free Europe; Britain. After the retreat from Dunkirk and the French surrender, Hitler believed the war was practically over. The British, defeated and without European allies, would quickly seek peace.

On 16th July Hitler ordered that plans be made for the invasion of Britain. A month had passed since the defeat of France, yet Winston Churchill refused to even consider an armistice and prepared Britain for war on the home front.

An invasion would require control of the seas and skies, but the Kriegsmarine had been crippled in the Norwegian Campaign to an extent that it could not take on the Royal Navy's Home Fleet. If control of the skies could be won by the Luftwaffe, then the Royal Navy might be prevented from halting the invasion. The outcome of a war hinged, for the first time, upon the outcome of an air battle.

The German air assault began on the Channel itself, then Fighter Command's airfields in an attempt to rest control of Britain's skies from the RAF. Hitler himself had initially forbidden the deliberate bombing of London, but the bombing war inevitably escalated until, on 5th September, he ordered indiscriminate attacks on British cities, including London.

On 7th September four hundred bombers attacked by day and night. The focus of the Luftwaffe had shifted away from Fighter Command's airfields, giving the RAF a slim chance to recover.

SUNDAY 15TH SEPTEMBER 1940

At 11 Group Headquarters in Uxbridge Air Vice Marshal Keith Park had important guests; Winston Churchill and his wife. There was no significance to Churchill's visit, he was 'just passing' and thought he would call in. As Keith Park led his guests down the stairs to the operations room some fifty feet underground he tactfully pointed out to Winston that the ventilation system would not cope with his cigar smoke; he clenched his cigar, unlit, between his teeth as events unfolded. Park had been made privy to intelligence that an all-out attack was soon to come and there had been a lull in activity for over a week. As he ordered his squadrons into the air one after another he is reputed to have said, "This, I think is what we have been waiting for. I think that it is about to happen."

The scene was set for an epic battle.

One-by-one squadrons were brought to Stand By and then Readiness as the enemy forces were plotted on the ops table. By midday twenty-three fighter squadrons were airborne. The scale of the enemy attack was such that Park knew his pilots could not repulse it; London was in for a 'pasting'.

Piloting one of the Dornier 17s was 27 year old Oberleutnant Robert Zehbe of the bomber unit 1/KG76. Zehbe's crew were old hands and had successfully completed several raids, including Kenley on August 18th and London on September 7th, but this time things were not going well for them. One engine was giving trouble and they began to lag behind the formation; a vulnerable position as fighter pilots loved to pick off a straggler. Turning for home was a riskier option, for an ailing bomber chugging alone across the skies of Kent was a sitting duck. They were 500 yards behind the formation when the first fighter attack came just south of London. Flight Lieutenant Jefferies led his flight of 310 (Czech) Squadron into the fray

Air Vice Marshal Keith Park who organised the RAF's response to the Luftwaffe raid on September 15th as Churchill watched.

and set the Dornier's port engine on fire; then his less experienced Czech charges had their turn at the bomber. Pilots from 609 and 504 squadrons also seized on the opportunity of an easy kill and poured more gunfire into the hapless Dornier, yet still it limped on. Two of its crew baled out; Ludwig Armbruster at Sydenham and Leo Hammermeister at Dulwich. Crossing the Thames at Battersea six fighters were seen making repeated attacks. Finally Robert Zehbe abandoned the Dornier, leaving his

young gunner Gustav Hubel dead or mortally wounded in the stricken aircraft. A badly wounded Zehbe landed at Kennington, where was beaten up by civilians; he died later of injuries.

Left: Flt Lt Jerrard Jeffries DFC (centre) of 310 Squadron was the first to attack Oblt Robert Zehbe's Dornier 17.

Below: Dornier 17s of KG76 climb into the morning sky heading for London during the Battle of Britain.

One of the attacking pilots was 26 year old Sergeant Ray Holmes. Ray, known as 'Arty' after his initial R-T, was flying a Hurricane from 504 Squadron and his actions over London would propel him into the limelight then – and 64 years later.

Ray poses for the camera on the wing of his Hurricane.

THE PILOT'S STORY - AS REPORTED IN WAR ILLUSTRATED

And here is the story told by the pilot who brought the 'plane down at Victoria Station. He is a Sergeant Pilot from West Kirby, in Cheshire, and it was his first fight. After he had shot down the enemy machine he had to jump by parachute. He said:

"I was in the last section of my Squadron, and my Dornier victim took all that I had to give him. Bits flew off him and I broke away intending to turn and attack again. My windscreen was covered with black oil, and when I did attack again I think it must have been a different machine. Anyway, as soon as I fired a big flame shot up, and I must have got his petrol tanks.

"I broke away again, and turned to make a head-on attack on another Dornier, firing a burst straight into its cockpit. At first I thought a piece of the Dornier had flown off but then I saw it was a German baling out. I passed so near that I believe I touched the parachute.

Opposite page: Frames from a newsreel showing Oblt. Zehbe's Dornier (top three) and Ray Holmes' Hurricane (lower three) falling to earth).

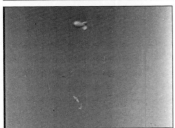

"As I made my final attack, my right wing struck something. I went into a terrific spin. There was no response from my controls.

"I flung the hood back and struggled to get out. I must have been doing well over 400 m.p.h. when I finally got out of the cockpit. The wind was so strong it was like a piece of an airplane hitting me. People on the ground told me later that my parachute opened at only three hundred feet.

"I spun across a house in Chelsea, got my feet down on a gutter, slid down the roof, and fell into the garden on my back. Then two girls came up to me, and I was so glad to see them that I kissed them both."

Ray Holmes landed in Hugh Street and, as soon he had his wits about him, he was borne off to a pub in Pimlico Road by the locals for a stiff brandy.

As the Dornier broke up its bombs fell, unarmed, over London. Two 50 kilo bombs fell in the grounds of Buckingham Palace, one on the palace's lawn. A shackle was found still attached to one of the bombs and was presented to the King. In the days before, several bombs had fallen on the palace and caused damage; now a bomber been brought down within sight of it. Soon journalists had hold of the story and, in its re-telling, the story became embroidered and elaborated upon. Soon the hero fighter pilot had deliberately rammed the German moments before it dropped its deadly cargo on the Royal family – he had saved the King single-handed!

THE BBC REPORT

Just after mid-day on Sunday, September 15, one Hurricane brought down three German bombers over London. I was lucky enough to see part of the engagement.

Just after the alarm sounded I could hear the drone of several German bombers. Soon bombs began to fall, some of them rather uncomfortably near. And then came a terrific rattle of machine-gun fire. I looked up in time to see one of our fighters weaving about among the bombers just under the clouds. Suddenly there was a terrific crash in the air as the Hurricane's guns found the bomb racks of one of the Germans. The German seemed just to disintegrate in the air. Two big pieces - the engines of the 'plane - hurtled down to earth, and bits and pieces floated down after them.

Soon after the German was hit there was a terrific screaming roar as a 'plane came hurtling down. At first I thought it was a dive bomber, but the crash told how the machine had hit the ground. It was the Hurricane, but the pilot, as it turned out, was safe.

By the time I reached the spot where the Hurricane had crashed, there wasn't much to see just a heap of tangled aluminium on the pavement, and a hole in the road from which you could see the back part of the engine sticking out, but there was still less to be seen of the German bomber, a part of which had fallen about a quarter of a mile farther on.

Edward Ward – BBC radio reporter

The Hurricane had indeed dived almost vertically to earth. Narrowly missing buildings it smashed through the roadway at the junction of Buckingham Palace Road and Ebury Bridge Road. The force of the impact broke-up the road's surface and ruptured water mains that flooded the junction. Within ten days this busy road junction was repaired, re-surfaced, and traffic rumbled over the site as if nothing had ever happened – for the next 64 years.

FINDING TM-B

Professional photographer Chris Bennett's imagination had been fired by the legend of this, the most famous single event in the Battle of Britain, many years before. A veteran of several aircraft excavations, Chris was adamant that there would be some evidence of Ray's Hurricane under the road. Finding an aircraft wreck in a field was one thing, but no one had ever attempted to find a wreck under a public road, and one of the busiest roads in London at that. Clearly, if any attempt were to be made to find TM-B a great deal of finance and organisation would be required.

Sgt Holmes
J15/43

SECRET. FORM "F."

COMBAT REPORT.

Sector Serial No.	(A)	
Serial No. of Order detailing Flight or Squadron to Patrol	(B)	
Date	(C)	15.9.1940
Flight, Squadron	(D)	Flight : Sqdn. : 504.
Number of Enemy Aircraft	(E)	About 20
Type of Enemy Aircraft	(F)	D.O.215s.
Time Attack was delivered	(G)	1210
Place Attack was delivered	(H)	Over London.
Height of Enemy	(J)	20,000
Enemy Casualties	(K)	1 D.O.215 destroyed. 1 D.O.215 damaged.
Our Casualties Aircraft	(L)	1 Hurricane Missing, One
Searchlights N(1) N/A. A.A.Guns Assistance N(11) NIL Personnel	(M)	Cat.two and One Cat.Thre P/O.Gurteen missing.
	(P)	No clear recollection
GENERAL REPORT.	(R)	

In the attack made by No.504 Squadron I attacked the right flank machine from quarter to astern. Pieces flew from the wings and a flame appeared in the port wing but went out again. After breaking away I climbed up to a single D.O.215 and made two quarter attacks. Pieces flew off. My windscreen was now splashed with black oil. I attacked a third time and a members of the crew baled out. On my fourth attack from the port beam a jar shook my starboard wing as I passed over the E/A and I went into an uncontrollable spin. I think the E/A must have exploded beneath me. I baled out and as I landed I saw the Dornier hit the ground by Victoria Street Station ½ mile away.

Signature R.T. Holmes Sgt.

O.C. { *Section* Green *Flight* B *Squadron* 504 Squadron No.

This panorama was created from a ten second clip of motion picture film taken by the fire brigade. It was the most vital piece of photographic evidence and without it the dig would not have happened. The wooden blocks that made up the road surface have been lifted up by the crash and water is running from the fractured main.

Fortunately Chris had worked closely with the production company behind the TimeTeam series and his photographs illustrate several books detailing the digs carried out for the programme. Perhaps TM-B would make a good show? Unfortunately the practicalities of the excavation were just too daunting and the idea was shelved. Over the next few years Chris pressed on with his plan and his research. Everyone wanted to know exactly where the 'plane lay; and what would be left of it underground, questions that Chris could not answer with certainty. Perhaps the BBC would be interested? Meeting followed meeting and months turned to years. Westminster Council had no objection, in principle, to an excavation; so long as their appointed highways contractor would carry out the work, and re-surface the road. How much? Only 30 or 40 thousand pounds! Then there were the other utilities, water, electricity, gas, telephones and the police. And what about the traffic? Victoria coach station was just around the corner and any diversion would have to take account of the new bendy-busses with their extra large turning radius.

Finally the idea came to the attention of the London based TV production company Mentorn, and particularly the presenter / producer Edwina Silver. 'Ed' managed to interest the British TV broadcaster Channel 5, but there was a catch; they wanted it broadcast 'live'. With potential sponsorship now in place the effort to pin down the site and any buried wreckage was re-doubled. Any site visit or survey had to be made in the early hours to minimise the disruption to traffic, thus a series of experts and their equipment made the rendezvous with Chris and project co-director Steve Vizard in the half light of many an early dawn. Ground penetrating radar identified many linear anomalies, such as utilities, but could not pin down anything that might be wreckage. A dowser brought his hazel twigs, but was unable to divine where the Merlin lay. Thames Water produced their plans of pipes and sewer tunnels and searched their archives for any record of the repairs made in 1940. Then, working on the assumption that the sewer may have been damaged by the crash, Thames Water assisted in underground surveys of the tunnels to look for repaired damage, but there was none. Coloured dye was poured down manholes and revealed only a pipe that the water company had no record of at all. A mysterious manhole cover on the junction resisted all efforts open it. When, finally, the cover was dug up it concealed only an abandoned section of sewer.

The only indisputable evidence of the precise location was photographic. The London Fire Brigade had filmed the incident and, crucially, taken still photographs from a different angle. If the positions of both camera men could be determined and lined up with surviving parts of the buildings then two lines could be drawn on a plan of the junction and, where the lines intersected, the wreck would be found. X really would mark the spot.

With less than a week to go before the live broadcast a final make-or-break meeting was held. Twenty-six people, representatives from all interested parties, gathered. The questions were the usual ones; what was left and where was it? The

The aerial photograph used to fix the impact spot of Ray's Hurricane using the Fire Brigade images.

The services and the predicted location.

The original and revised location (shown in blue) of the hole after the water main forced a change.

entire venture hinged on the decision of project manager Chris Bennett and his X on the map; to go and take a gamble, or abandon the project for ever. But at the last moment another complication arose. The theoretical location had been painstakingly worked out, but a large water main was known to run through the spot. This was presumably the repaired water pipe; but if the wreckage turned out to be directly under the pipe it would have to stay where it was for fear of damaging the water main. The maximum size of the hole was 3 metres square and it had to drop down directly over the crash site, the sides could not be under-mined. If the hole 'missed' the target by only 50 centimetres it would not be recovered. Crucially, to avoid the water main, Chris was obliged to shift the position of his hole away from his preferred position by two metres. The odds against a successful dig were stacking up rapidly and time was running out. Chris's agonising decision was a 'go'.

The excavation was to take place over the May bank holiday weekend. The site was to be

prepared on Saturday, ready to film the final stages of the excavation 'live' under floodlights on Sunday. On Monday the site would be re-instated, ready to the re-open in time for the Tuesday morning rush hour.

On Saturday 29th May 2004 the road diversions were put in place, contractor's staff and plant were on site, power laid on to the site offices, and the television outside broadcast facilities assembled.

The scene on Sunday morning, before the show, with machinery, outside-broadcast trucks and traffic diversion in place.

After years of planning a Barhale disk cutter finally sliced into the tarmac of Ebury Bridge Road.

As today's road surface was removed and taken from the site the first tiny fragments of TM-B appeared; a tiny length of rubber tube and piece of aluminium smaller than a postage stamp. As the excavation became deeper more finds appeared, mixed with wood and tar blocks that had made up the 1940 road surface. The relief was palpable.

THE PILOT

Neither Chris nor Steve Vizard had met TM-B's pilot, Ray Holmes. Edwina and the production company 'Mentorn' were keen that he should be involved in the broadcast, but his poor health was thought to preclude his travelling to London.

Instead an outside broadcast link was to be provided to his Merseyside home, where he could watch the action in London and a reporter and crew could capture his reaction. Only days before the broadcast Ray had a doctor's appointment and the subject came into the conversation; Remarkably, the doctor's view was that, with the correct medical supervision, Ray would be able to go to London; if he wished.

Again the carefully laid plans were thrown into confusion and it was decided that Ray would be re-united with past and present members of his squadron in the Orange Brewery, where he had been taken in 1940.

A valve and con-rod from the shattered Merlin engine.

Ray Holmes, enjoying a pint at the Orange Brewery where he had been taken in 1940.

John Suchet, the co-presenter with Edwina Silver, at the bottom of the hole where a lifting strop has been attached to the engine.

Below: The engine slowly emerges from the hole.

By Sunday afternoon everyone involved was in buoyant mood; the main wreckage had been found only two metres from the centre of the excavation and just at the edge of the water main. The critical water main ran so close to the engine that some parts were actually embedded in the concrete foundation. Satisfyingly for Chris, the engine was dead-centre of his planned excavation as proposed before he had to move it to avoid the water main. At 9 o'clock on Sunday evening the opening credits rolled and the 'live' Channel 5 broadcast began. The whole site was lit by powerful lights against the dark night. A huge crowd had gathered behind the safety barriers to see the spectacle and still more looked on with binoculars from vantage points on the surrounding buildings.

Right on cue the battered Rolls-Royce Merlin engine

of Ray Holmes' Hurricane was lifted clear of the hole amid cheers from the crowd. But there were a couple of twists to the night still left. Team leader Steve Vizard was sifting through the spoil at the bottom of the shaft in the semi-darkness when he came across TM-B's control column; almost unrecognisable in the twisted instrument panel. Delighted at the unbelievable find, Steve dashed across to where Chris and Edwina were chatting – and into over 2 million homes – the interview was going out live.

Finally, just as things were winding down, a spontaneous cheer erupted from the crowd; heads turned to see Ray Holmes appear out of the darkness into the bright camera lights. Flanked by his wife and son, Ray Holmes had made it back to the Hurricane he had left 64 years before.

The Merlin engine and some other parts of TM-B were exhibited at the temporary exhibition 'Westminster at War' and then at the Imperial War Museum. Some of the broken and unrecognisable engine parts were later turned into miniature replicas of Ray Holmes' Hurricane by Chris Bennett's own company TMB Art Metal. Only 125 models were made, one was presented to Ray himself, another to The Queen and Prince Philip in a ceremony, appropriately enough, at Buckingham Palace.

Top left: Chris Bennett shows Ray the control column from his Hurricane.

Left: Chris Bennett and Steve Vizard presented The Queen with one of TMB Art Metal's models made from pieces of the Merlin.

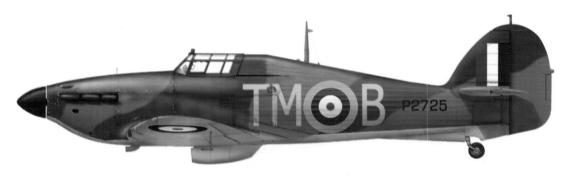

Above: Ray Holmes' Hurricane P2725 as it would have appeared on the day it fell to earth over London.

Left: The shattered Merlin engine from Ray's Hurricane on display at the Imperial War Museum.

THE 'RESERVE' DIG

Until the very last moment the outcome of the dig in the centre of London was in doubt, but the Channel 5 broadcast was called 'Fighter Dig - Live' and a dig there would be. Had the excavation of TM-B failed, a back-up dig had been organised in Germany by TV producer James Cutler. Again the excavation was carried out 'live' and veteran TimeTeam member Guy de le Bédoyère would present it with Spitfire restorer John Romain and the aircraft's pilot, Vic Murphy, who had been flown from Australia. The subject was Spitfire XIV RN203 of 130 Squadron, 125 Wing, that Vic had baled out of in 1945 at Schwerinsee, east of Hamburg.

On April 19th, 1945 Vic made a sortie over enemy airfields in Northern Germany. His four-plane section found itself attacked and outnumbered by a formation of FW190s that, he suspected, were factory-fresh because they had no camouflage.

He reported:

"I was in a steep turn attacking an FW190 when I saw another FW190 firing at me, but as his angle off was 60 degrees I did not think he could hit me. But then my engine cut and I caught fire, so he must have hit me. I baled out and landed south of Wittenburg."

Within minutes Vic was captured by German soldiers and marched to Wittenburg where an officer interrogated him. His confinement in a variety of PoW camps lasted only a month - until he was liberated by British troops.

He returned to Australia with his wife Ria who had served in the Royal Canadian Air Force and eventually he became an estate agent in Queensland.

Sitting quietly on a plastic garden-chair watching the excavator recover the wreckage of his Spitfire, Vic explained that everything came back to him, every picture, every second, every detail.

Ray Holmes - One of The Few

Raymond Towers Holmes was born on 20th August 20 1914 at Wallasey, Cheshire. His father was a journalist, a career he would follow. At Grammar School he excelled at sport, but then followed his father and became a crime reporter. In 1937 he joined the RAFVR as an airman pilot and on completion of his training was posted to 504 Squadron in June 1940. Early in September, at the height of the Battle of Britain, his squadron moved from Scotland to Hendon and was thrown into battle.

Following Ray's escapades on 15th September he was commissioned in June 1941. He then moved with his squadron (re-numbered as 81 Squadron) to Murmansk, northern Russia. He flew on operations until November, when the squadron left its planes to the Russians and returned to England.

Ray Holmes then spent two years an instructor at a fighter OTU before becoming a Spitfire reconnaissance pilot. He left the RAF in 1945 and went back journalism in Liverpool. At the age of 80 he retired from being a Crown Court reporter. He had become an institution in court circles, always taking meticulous notes with a fountain pen in perfect shorthand and mentoring younger journalists in the ways of the court.

In 2004 the Wirral Borough Council bestowed the Freedom of the Borough on Holmes, the chief executive said, "he could think of no one upon whom this honour could have been more fittingly bestowed".

Ray died from cancer on 27th June 2005. On the day he died, flags in the Wirral flew at half-mast in his honour and his widow, Anne, received a message from Buckingham Palace expressing the Queen's sadness on hearing of his death.

WHO DOWNED DOUGLAS BADER?

CHANNEL 4

FIRST SHOWN AUGUST 2006

DIRECTOR: SIMON RAIKES

PRODUCED BY: WILDFIRE TV

WHO DOWNED DOUGLAS BADER?

B ader was born in north London in 1910, but soon went to India. He returned to England to attend school and excelled at sport, particularly rugby and cricket, and may have played for England had things turned out different. He was then successful in winning a place at the RAF college Cranwell and graduated in 1930 to fly fighters with No.23 Squadron. His story may well have ended on 14 December 1931 when he crashed his Bristol Bulldog during a low-level aerobatic demonstration. His injuries were nearly fatal and he lost both legs, but he survived. There was no place for a legless pilot in the RAF and so he was invalided out and took a job with a petrol company.

When war broke out he began his campaign to be reinstated in the RAF as a pilot. His determination and contacts won him a flying test and finally he joined No.19 Squadron as a Flying Officer flying Spitfires. His next promotion was to flight commander with 222 Squadron and in July 1940 he was given command of 242 Squadron, flying Hurricanes.

Bader was a firm believer in the 'Big Wing' tactic where several squadrons would form a single formation to take on the enemy in strength. March 1941 saw the 'legless Ace' appointed Wing

Commander Flying of the Tangmere Wing – the first Wing Leader. He led fighter sweeps across the Channel to engage the Luftwaffe over their own airfields. After claiming 20 enemy aircraft destroyed and more damaged or probable in just over a year of combat, he did not return from an operation over France on August 9th 1941. He spent the rest of the war in captivity, part of the time, famously, in Colditz Castle.

Back in the RAF he led the Battle of Britain flypast over London in 1945 and finally left the RAF in 1946 to go back to his job with Shell. His biography 'Reach for the Sky' was made into a film, with Kenneth More in the role of Bader, and he became a household name. In his last years he used his celebrity status to promote charities for the disabled until his death from a heart attack in 1982 at the age of 72.

THE BADER MYSTERY

With a legendary personality such as Bader, as with Dambuster Guy Gibson, it is little wonder that there is an enduring fascination with all aspects of the man and his exploits. Among Bader aficionados there was one question that defied a definitive answer; how was he brought down over France in August 1941?

Andy Saunders had pondered this conundrum since the early 1970s and had corresponded with and interviewed many of the key figures. An historian, excavator of aircraft and founder of the Tangmere Museum, Andy was ideally placed to take up the challenge of providing the solution.

CIRCUS 68 - 9 AUGUST 1941

By August 1941 the RAF was taking the fight to the Luftwaffe. By sending small forces of bombers over France to tempt the German fighter pilots into the air it was hoped to engage them in combat. The targets for these 'Circus' sorties were often not of great value and the bomber force a token effort, as was the case on Circus 68. Just five Blenheim bombers were ordered to attack a power station at Gosnay – escorting the five bombers were 180 Spitfires!

The fighter 'Wings' each made up of three squadrons, came from North Weald, Hornchurch, Kenley, Northolt and Tangmere to rendezvous over Manston on the Kent coast, before heading across the Channel.

The carefully laid plans allocated each wing, each squadron and each pilot a place and a role. Bader was to lead the Tangmere Wing and direct the wing's operations as Target Support while flying with 616 Squadron. Wing Commander Bader's number two – his 'escort' was a lowly New Zealand Sergeant pilot called Jeff West who took the place of the usual number two who was not flying because he had a cold. Alongside 616 Squadron was 610 Squadron and above them should have been 41 Squadron, but it was late and could not catch the rest up to fulfil its role of protecting them from attack from above.

The armada crossed the coast and headed for the target, but a layer of cloud below prevented the bombers finding their main target. Turning back for home the bombs

were dropped harmlessly in fields and the sea near Fort Phillipe. The bombers' close escort wing and top cover wing saw little action and returned, but the German fighters attacked the Target Support Wings, including the Tangmere Wing.

The situation at 24,000 feet (4 ½ miles high) was confused as 180 Spitfire pilots tried to spot a few attacking Messerschmitts – that looked not dissimilar to Spitfires! Eventually a group of 17 Me109s below them was pointed out to Bader by Flight Lieutenant Roy Marples. Seeing the opportunity to catch them Bader called to Jeff West, 'Stay with me' and dived onto the Messerschmitts. Jeff West recalled the moment to Andy Saunders:

"There were about seventeen Me109s coming up and Douglas said. 'Righto chaps, we're going down'. Well, the four of us went down – Douglas, me on his left, and Dundas on his right with Johnson to the right of him. We flew in a finger-four pattern. Anyway, I think he was tired and anxious at this stage. I wouldn't have attacked from that height because we were about 5,000 feet above them and we were screaming down at full throttle around 450 mph. When we came out I was just ready to press the titty and I thought Douglas had picked the same one as I had so I thought I'd look for another one. The one on the left pulled up into a screaming turn and I thought. Ah, I'll go after him 'cos I had all the speed in the world. The other 109s all turned on their backs and dived away and I think Douglas kept following the same 109 down. When I went up I nearly rammed it and I could see the pilot slumped in the cockpit after I had shot at it. I thought, 'My God, I've killed some mother's son'. Almost at once I was in a spin, and when I came out of it there was nothing in sight. Nothing. Nothing."

Some of the pilots involved in Circus 68. Sitting centre is Cocky Dundas, standing is Nip Heppell and on the right is Bill Burton - the commanding officer of 616 Squadron.

Opposite; One of 'Buck' Casson's earlier Spitfires, P7753. He was shot down in this aircraft over Sussex on 5 May 1941. By August 1941 616 Squadron had changed its code letters from QJ to YQ.

Blue Section of 616 Squadron followed these four down. Leading Blue Section was Flight Lieutenant Lionel 'Buck' Casson who saw the Spitfires attack then break away to port. He fired at a pair of Me109s, but then diverted his attention to a lone fighter. He fired nearly all his ammunition at this aircraft. Most of the tail was shot away and eventually the pilot baled out at 6,000 feet.

Pilot Office Heppell attacked an Me109 and saw the pilot come out of the cockpit and fall into the cloud far below, but the pilot's parachute never opened and he fell - turning over and over as he went.

The 616 Squadron pilots now began to work their way out of the engagement and climbed whilst joining up into a small group. Two Me109s made repeated attacks from above and each time the group turned and their attackers broke off, only to repeat the performance. 'Buck' Casson sighted what he took for a damaged Spitfire below him and went down to offer assistance, assuming the Me109s had followed the formation as they were nowhere to be seen. Unfortunately for Buck Casson, the Messerschmitt pilots were following him. One of the Me109s was being flown by the Luftwaffe 'Ace' Gerhard Schoepfel who finally sent a cannon shell through Casson's cockpit and into the engine. Casson had no option but to crash land and was soon a prisoner of the Germans.

Left is Roy Marples, who pointed out the Me109s to Bader, and right is 'Buck' Casson.

On his way back over the Channel, Jeff West realised that he had lost Bader. *"I thought: Oh my God, I have lost the bloody CO".*

The Lost Spitfires of Circus 68 - 9 August 1941

Spitfire Va W3185 'Lord Lloyd' flying with 616 Squadron.
Wing Commander D R S Bader DSO DFC baled out and taken prisoner at Boeseghem.
Aircraft believed crashed near Mont Dupil Farm, between Racquinghem and Blaringhem.

Spitfire Vb W3458 'Mirfield' 616 Squadron.
Flight Lieutenant L H Casson DFC crash landed and taken prisoner at Les Attaques.

Spitfire IIA P7682 452 Squadron.
Pilot Officer J H O'Byrne (RAAF) baled out and taken prisoner at Coubronne.
Aircraft believed crashed NNW of Coubronne.

Spitfire IIA P7590 452 Squadron.
Sergeant G B Chapman killed when his aircraft crashed near Salperwick.

Spitfire IIA P8361 'Krakatoa' 452 Squadron.
Sergeant G B Haydon baled out but fell dead at Quercamps. Aircraft crashed at Forêt de Tournehem.

The Spitfires that crashed near St Omer

9 August 1941
Spitfire Va W3185 'Lord Lloyd' flying with 616 Squadron.
Wing Commander D R S Bader DSO DFC baled out and taken prisoner at Boeseghem.
Aircraft believed crashed near Mont Dupil Farm, between Racquinghem and Blaringhem.

9 August 1941
Spitfire IIA P7682 452 Squadron.
Pilot Officer J H O'Byrne (RAAF) baled out and taken prisoner at Coubronne.
Aircraft believed crashed NNW of Coubronne.

9 August 1941
Spitfire IIA P7590 452 Squadron.
Sergeant G B Chapman killed when his aircraft crashed near Salperwick.

9 August 1941
Spitfire IIA P8361 'Krakatoa' 452 Squadron.
Sergeant G B Haydon baled out but fell dead at Quercamps. Aircraft crashed at Forêt de Tournehem.

8 June 1942
Spitfire Vb BM303 611 Squadron
Sergeant J E Misseldine baled out and escaped capture. Aircraft crashed at Blaringhem.

25 November 1943
Spitfire IX MA764 MT-L 122 Squadron
Flight Sergeant D Bostock baled out and escaped capture - he was hidden for a time at Mont Dupil Farm.
Aircraft believed crashed at Racquinghem.

Unknown
Unidentified Spitfire IX.
Unknown pilot killed.
Aircraft crashed at Boeseghem.

THE DIGS

THE MYSTERY SPITFIRE

Unsurprisingly several researchers have been drawn into the mire that is the Bader Mystery. The first attempt from this side of the Channel was made by Dilip Sarkar in 1996. Amidst great interest from the British press the site of a Spitfire crash at Les Clies, Boeseghem was excavated by Dilip and the Malvern Spitfire Team. The site had been identified as that of Bader's crash by a local French researcher and was certainly within the area of probability. The Daily Telegraph published a report on the excavation in January 1996 and declared, 'Douglas Bader's Spitfire found in French Field'. In May 1996 The Times reported that the team were, 'almost certain' that the wreck was that of Bader's aircraft.

Although locals firmly believed this to be Bader's Spitfire, the parts recovered showed it to have been a Mk.IX and therefore it could not have been; it had cannons (not machineguns) a Merlin 66 engine (not Merlin 45) a 4 blade (not a 3 blade) propeller. A wrist watch and the 'D-Ring' to the parachute were also found, evidence enough that the pilot had been killed in the crash. So far the aircraft and its unfortunate pilot have defied conclusive identification.

Following the death of 'Buck' Casson, one of the main participants in the combat, in 2003 speculation began to mount that Casson had shot down Bader during the dogfight. The evidence was sketchy, but it would make a great headline should a newspaper seek to sensationalise an incident that was at worst only an unfortunate mistake in the heat of combat. Andy Saunders therefore decided to reopen his file on the incident in an effort to lay the matter to rest once and for all.

SCHLAGER'S ME109

Key to the mystery was the fate of Unteroffizier Albert Schlager and his Messerschmitt – the only one lost in the combat. 'Buck' Casson had made it abundantly clear that he had fired almost all his ammunition at an Me109, its tail had come off and the pilot had baled out. Fellow squadron member 'Nip' Heppell also reported shooting down an Me109 and reported that its pilot had fallen to his death with an unopened parachute. Both claims were made at the approximate time and place where Bader and Schlager had been shot down and killed. The question was; which account best fitted the circumstances of Schlager's loss?

An aircraft crash site that was believed to have been that of Schlager's Me109 was pointed out by a French researcher, and an excavation arranged for June 2004. The questions that the excavation would seek to answer were:

Was this the right aircraft?
Had its tail been shot off?
Had the pilot been killed in the aircraft, or had he fallen to his death?

The crash site in a meadow at Aire-sur-La-Lys had been identified by Georges Goblet; the very same man who had led the Malvern Spitfire Team to 'Bader's Spitfire' seven years earlier. Was he right this time?

The excavation proved both expensive and frustrating. It soon became clear that the aircraft had dived into the soft ground at terrific speed and had buried itself almost completely. By midday only a few small fragments, undeniably from an Me109, had surfaced. In spite of the size of the excavator the main wreckage, and the answers, remained tantalising out of reach. Fired with enthusiasm, the French contractor offered to provide a second, still bigger, digger; but it would cost a second day's hire, and a low-loader transporter to move it and the driver. Not wanting to be beaten it was decided to 'go for broke'.

In the stifling heat of a summer afternoon the dig continued. The hole rapidly got bigger and deeper, yet the bulk of the wreck remained just out of reach and had to be abandoned. Remarkably the few parts found were sufficient to answer Andy's questions. A

manufacturer's label just centimetres long bore the aircraft's Werke Nummer '8350' confirming that this was indeed Schlager's Me109. A fragment from the Swastika that had been painted on the tail and the tail wheel were evidence enough that the tail had been largely intact when the aircraft had crashed and had not been 'shot off'. Finally there was no evidence, by way a parachute or anything else, that the pilot had died in the wreck; he had baled out, but had fallen to his death.

Everything pointed to this being the Messerschmitt that Pilot Officer Heppell had reported shooting down.

Paul Cole with the tail wheel from Schlager's Me109 - proving that this was Nip Heppell's victim.

Despite the scale of the excavation it proved impossible to reach the main wreck of the Me109, but sufficient evidence of the tail had been found.

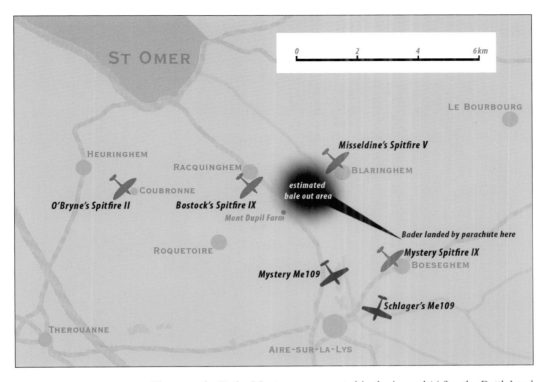

ST OMER

0   2   4   6km

LE BOURBOURG

Misseldine's Spitfire V

HEURINGHEM

RACQUINGHEM   BLARINGHEM

COUBRONNE

estimated
bale out area

O'Bryne's Spitfire II   *Bostock's Spitfire IX*

Mont Dupil Farm

Bader landed by parachute here

ROQUETOIRE   *Mystery Spitfire IX*
                           BOESEGHEM

Mystery Me109

Schlager's Me109

THEROUANNE

AIRE-SUR-LA-LYS

The story the Bader Mystery was reported in the journal 'After the Battle' and picked up by the 'Mail on Sunday' in August 2004. The TV documentary production company 'Wildfire' had been taking a keen interest in the story and obtained a commission from Channel 4 to make a two hour 'special' entitled 'Who Downed Douglas Bader?' The programme would explore Bader as a person as well as the mystery surrounding his last combat. The 'Wildfire' production team have a long association with archaeology having been engaged in making regular episodes of TimeTeam and TimeTeam specials. With extra resources available new avenues of investigation opened. Retired air crash investigator Bernie Forward was called upon to independently look into the evidence of Bader's loss and to identify a likely area for the crash site. Meteorologist Jim Allen was to investigate the weather and winds at the time of the combat. Between them they could back-track the course of Bader's parachute from where he landed to the point in the sky where he had baled out – beneath that point in the sky would lie his Spitfire's crash site. Appeals for information about the crash were broadcast and printed in local newspapers and a short-list of three possible sites drawn up; two near Racquinghem and one near Blaringhem.

On a freezing October day in 2005 a combined team of specialists brought in by Wildfire and aircraft hunters assembled by Andy Saunders met in their temporary HQ at Mont Dupil Farm, Racquinghem, in the centre of the search area. An RAF

fighter pilot, Donald Bostock, had been hidden from Germans at this very farm after he had baled out of his Spitfire. A newspaper article published in 1945 reported that the aircraft of the famous legless British pilot had crashed here and there were stories that an artificial leg had been found in fields nearby. Finally Monsieur Duhamel, the current farmer, whose father had hidden Bostock believed that Bader's plane had fallen just behind the farm buildings.

Andy Saunders (right) puts his evidence to crash investigator Bernie Forward at Mont Dupil Farm.

The investigation over the next four days was to be split into four phases:

1/ A search by massed metal detectors of the zone directly beneath Bader's calculated bale out point.

2/ A thorough grid search of the field at Mont Dupil Farm where Monsieur Duhamel indicated that a plane had crashed and the where the 'leg' was reportedly found.

3/ An excavation at the crash site at Blaringhem.

4/ An excavation at the second crash site at Racquinghem.

The search under the bale out point failed to find anything aircraft related and locals who lived there during the war could not recall anything crashing in that area. Having ruled out the scientifically calculated area, the focus of the search switched to Mont Dupil Farm itself. Monsieur Duhamel was able to pinpoint the point where the plane had fallen accurately and aerial photographs showed the trees that he remembered the wreck being laying against. Surely there must be some evidence of the crash? Never had the search team been to a site like this, where an aircraft had crashed with the violence that Bader's obviously had, and found absolutely nothing. Regular TimeTeam member Kerry Ely organised a grid search of the field and each metal object was plotted, but not one thing was from an aircraft. But Monsieur Duhamel did recall that the aircraft was little damaged, was not buried and had not caught fire! How, then, could this be Bader's aircraft that had its tail shot off and had dived almost vertically into the ground? The chance of finding a third crash site in the area that might be Bader's Spitfire had been reduced to almost zero. This left two crash sites and three Spitfires. Although local researcher Georges Goblet had suggested the identities of the two sites there was no conclusive evidence to prove it. The spectre of the Malvern Spitfire Team's mis-identification loomed large - it was time to examine the wrecks.

The 'crash site' at Mont Dupil Farm where it was believed Bader's Spitfire had fallen - yet not a trace was found.

THE BLARINGHEM SPITFIRE

The site was immediately adjacent to the road from Blaringhem to Sercus and after an examination of a war-time aerial reconnaissance photograph it was initially feared that road widening might have encompassed the site. Eventually a few fragments were located on the field margin; the road-side ditch stopped just short the crash site. The film crew and excavator shifted location from the farm and the first excavation of the expedition got underway. It was not an auspicious start. It immediately became apparent that the aircraft had not dived into the ground at any great speed, but had probably been in a spin of some sorts when it had struck the ground. Parts of the armoured glass windscreen appeared within the first metre and just below that the unusual spectacle of three wooden propeller blades neatly placed on top of each other in the bottom of the shallow impact crater. Very little of the airframe or engine remained, but there were enough clues to at least determine the mark of Spitfire – it was not Bader's.

The propeller blades that ruled this site out as Bader's Spitfire.

Sgt. John Misseldine, pilot of the Blaringhem Spitfire.

A photograph of Bader's Spitfire showed it fitted with de Havilland metal propeller blades, but wooden Rotol blades had been found. Further evidence came from the handful of fragments in the finds trays. Peter Arnold picked out a tiny component that he identified as part of the safely switch from inside the firing button of a cannon armed machine; 'Oh, I took one apart a few years ago', was his response to the legitimate question of how he came to identify such an obscure thing! Later a brass bezel from the clock fitted to the instrument panel was identified as being from a type of clock not yet in use at the time of Bader's crash.

It was concluded that the Blaringhem Spitfire was a Mark Vb, serial BM303 of 611 Squadron. It had been lost on 8th June 1942 when Sergeant J E Misseldine had been shot down and baled out. Jack Misseldine was flying his first combat sortie when he was brought down. He baled out with burns to his face and minor injuries and was hidden by locals. Eventually a doctor tended to his injuries and he was helped on his way to Gibraltar, from where he returned to England in September 1942. In July 2007 Andy Saunders presented Jack with the brass bezel from the clock that had been found in the wreck of his aircraft.

THE RACQUINGHEM SPITFIRE

While filming continued at a number of other locations a party set off to search for the crash site that was believed to be a couple of kilometres north-west of Mont Dupil. After many hours of fruitless searching it became clear that the aircraft had not crashed in the field that had been pointed out by an eye-witness. Time was running out, with one day's filming left. Much of that evening was spent in heated discussion on how best to spend the final day. It seemed more than likely that this was Spitfire Mark IX, serial MA764 that Flight Sergeant D Bostock had escaped from after he was shot down on 25th November 1943, but there was a chance that another mis-identification had been made. The question was; could the programme's producer risk the possibility of it being Bader's after all? Finally the decision was made to find and excavate the site. The following morning the search area was widened to include neighbouring fields and a few parts, unmistakably from an aircraft, were found in a hedgerow. Specialist deep-seeking equipment pinpointed the main impact point in a field a hundred metres or so from the first finds, it seemed that a lot of Spitfire was still buried beneath the field.

The excavator was urgently summoned once again from Mont Dupil just as the fickle weather played its final trick and produced a rainstorm. Project leader Andy Saunders and one of the film crews had meanwhile set off to film in St Omer, leaving Paul Cole in charge of a tricky archaeo-salvage operation. As the rain beat down the topsoil was adeptly stripped off to reveal the outline of the impact crater, but very little metal. Traces of disturbance indicated that the first wreckage was over a metre below the surface and the digger's bucket sliced through the heavy clay. Without warning a large slab of clay peeled away to reveal part of the fuselage side and fuel tank that instantly gushed its high octane petrol into the hole. The anaerobic conditions created when the impervious clay had entombed the Spitfire more than sixty years before had preserved everything. Extraordinarily, the fragile roundel on the fuselage had been perfectly preserved and its colours were as bright as the day they were painted; but instantly revealed that this was not Bader's machine. The roundel featured a yellow outer ring of a style not in use during 1941, this was a Spitfire from a later in the war.

Under the competent leadership of Paul Cole the centre section and cockpit was lifted from the hole in a single, huge, digger bucket full. All the wreckage was put into bulk delivery bags for later cleaning and sorting, but among the shattered airframe and ancillary components were found the pilot's flying helmet and goggles. In the pilot's hurry to get out he had chosen to tear off his helmet rather

Excavation leader Paul Cole shows off the fuselage roundel, the first evidence that this was not Bader's Spitfire either!

Opposite top;
Flt. Sgt. Donald Bostock, pilot of Spitfire MA764 that crashed at Racquinghem.

Opposite right:
Bostock's battered helmet with initials painted on the leather. It's probably a good thing that this item wasn't found first...

than unplug the oxygen pipe and headphone lead. Still plainly visible on top the leather helmet were the owner's initials – DB – not Douglas Bader, but Donald Bostock.

Ample evidence was available from the large quantity of well preserved wreckage to positively identify this Spitfire as MA764. Flight Sergeant Bostock had been flying with 122 Squadron when his aircraft had been hit by an unlucky round that punctured a glycol pipeline. Deprived of its coolant the Merlin engine overheated and finally caught fire, leaving the pilot no choice other than to take to his parachute. Bostock landed in the grounds of Mont Dupil and was hidden by Monsieur Duhamel, father of the present owner, in the very outbuildings that the team were filming in. Less than two months later Bostock arrived back in England, having escaped via Gibraltar with the help of the French underground.

Back in the UK the remains of MA764 were re-assembled on a wooden framework for the purposes of filming. Donald Bostock passed away in 1984, but his widow, Alma, was contacted and invited to see her late husband's aircraft. Finally, in a fitting end to exceptionally long project, Andy Saunders presented Alma with Donald's flying helmet and goggles. 'It was', said Andy, 'a particularly moving moment and the most rewarding aspect of the entire endeavour'.

The assembled wreck of MA764. The airframe has been allocated the UK civil registration G-MCDB with the intention of rebuilding it.

Wildfire and Channel 4 had taken on an ambitious challenge, to resolve a mystery that had previously defeated many others. The question of 'Who Downed Douglas Bader?' had been answered; an unfortunate 'own goal' by one of Bader's own pilots. Where Bader's Spitfire fell was also resolved. It was certainly not one of the sites excavated. The Wildfire documentary ended by posing the theory that his Spitfire had fallen in an area that had been turned into lake, but subsequent research indicated that this aircraft was probably an Me109. The most likely conclusion is that W3185 disintegrated in the air over Mont Dupil and that parts fell like a shower of confetti over a wide area. In cases such as this it would be expected that the engine and nose, weighing over a ton, would bury itself to some extent, but the wings and rear fuselage would flutter down to be easily removed. There is a recollection that an engine fell at the Desprez sawmill, close to Mont Dupil, perhaps on the mill buildings themselves. Whether or not this is the case and whether or not it was Bader's engine is perhaps academic, the important point is that the mystery of Bader's last fight had been solved.

Full details can be found in 'Bader's Last Fight' by Andy Saunders, published by Grub Street in 2007.

Background painting by Mark Postlethwaite shows Douglas Bader in combat over the French coast in 1941.

THE LAST OF THE DAMBUSTERS

CHANNEL 5 / THE HISTORY CHANNEL

FIRST SHOWN JUNE 2008

DIRECTORS:

JAMES CUTLER AND CY CHADWICK

PRODUCED BY ATYPICAL MEDIA

THE LAST OF THE DAMBUSTERS

In 1943 the RAF's most modern bomber was the 22 ton, Rolls Royce Merlin powered, Avro Lancaster. When plans were being made to bomb the dams in Germany to flood and disrupt Hitler's arms factories, the Lancaster was the obvious machine for the job. The basic aircraft needed extensive modifications to take Barnes Wallis's four-ton 'bouncing bomb' and the job was given to the makers just two months before the raid was to take place. The cost to modify 23 aircraft was £6,274 and the now top-secret bombers were given the strange name, 'Type 464 Provisioning' Lancaster. The type number came from Vickers (who produced the weapon and dropping gear) while the addition of the word 'provisioning' was intended to show that the modifications were provisional, allowing the aircraft to be returned to standard configuration.

Two views of Lancaster ED825 photographed at Boscombe Down a few weeks before the Dambuster Raid.

The Lancaster that came to be the focus for the documentary had the RAF serial number ED825 and had been built at Avro's Woodford factory in Manchester. It was the third aircraft to be completed with the special 'Type 464 Provisioning'

Dambuster modifications. The first two aircraft (ED765 and ED817) were used in the dropping trials of the new weapon. ED825 however, was flown to the Aircraft and Armament Experimental Establishment at Boscombe Down for tests to determine how the modified aircraft would fly.

The main modifications included a new fairing over the front half of the bomb bay made of plywood over a wood frame (replacing the bomb bay doors), some V-shaped arms to carry the bomb, an under gunner's position and the removal of the mid-upper turret; these last two modifications were to become vital evidence on the dig. More minor changes included up-rated engines, a revised hydraulic and oil system, the removal of the de-icing equipment and balloon cable cutters on the leading edge of the wing, and a larger bomb aimer's blister.

In the month leading up to the raid a number of trials were carried out both with and without the bomb fitted. During one high-speed dive with the four-ton bomb fitted, parts of the plywood covering broke off, so this was replaced with Alclad sheeting, an aluminium-like material.

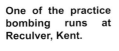

One of the practice bombing runs at Reculver, Kent.

By mid May 1943, the crews of 617 Squadron, which had been formed for the operation, had been training using their 'Type 464s' for several weeks. As the planned date for the raid approached, and despite the fact that two crews had been stood down through illness, the squadron still had no spare aircraft should one of the operational ones go unserviceable. Its tests completed, ED825 was flown to RAF Scampton for the squadron to prepare as a spare aircraft.

On May 16th 1943 (the day of the operation) Captain Bergel and Third Officer Salter of the Air Transport Auxiliary ferried '825 to Scampton, although Bergel noted that an engine was a little sluggish and would not run at full revs. Normally this would prevent such a flight but he decided not to worry about this as the aircraft was deemed 'Priority 1', and instead reported it to the ground crews, who set to work preparing the aircraft for the operation, 'just is case'. The mechanics worked on the engines, loaded a bomb and painted the code letters on the fuselage - AJ-T. The famous spotlights, a set of two lights that shone down to converge at a predetermined height above the water, thus giving the correct altitude, were not fitted because there was not enough time.

Later that night, as the crews prepared to start the engines, Flight Lieutenant McCarthy in his usual ED915 (AJ-Q) found that he had an engine problem. Remembering the spare ED825, and terrified that their weeks of training would be wasted, he and his crew dashed across the tarmac to claim it. In the process, one of the crew's parachutes caught on something and billowed open. Undeterred, McCarthy reached the Lancaster only to discover there was no compass deviation card, essential to navigate to and from the target. With minutes to spare the card and a spare parachute were found, and McCarthy took off for the Sorpe Dam.

The delay of around half an hour saw the crew take off at 22.01 hours, the last of their flight of five detailed to attack the Sorpe. During the outward flight the crew reported seeing several fighters above them and both gunners exchanged fire with Flak positions and shot out the searchlights. At one point, Sergeant Batson, the front gunner, asked for permission to open fire on a train only to discover it was a Flak train. The return fire hit the aircraft in the port undercarriage nacelle and burst the tyre.

**Joe McCarthy and his crew who took ED825 to the Sorpe Dam and back.
'Johnny' Johnson is on the left.**

The Sorpe Dam as it was in 1939. Langscheid and its prominent church is on the hill.

A photo taken on the morning after the raid showing the damaged crest.

The crew flew on to the Sorpe Dam, but upon reaching it at 00.15 hours found it to be shrouded in mist. McCarthy circled for a while before making his first run over the dam. The attacks made by Guy Gibson and the rest of the squadron at the Möhne and Eder dams required the bomb to be set spinning before it was dropped so that it would 'bounce' off the water until it hit the wall of the dam at right angles. The Sorpe Dam was built differently and for this the bomb had to be dropped along the length of the dam and not spinning. McCarthy made his bomb run over a hill on one side of the valley, dived down the hillside and levelled out to fly the 600 metres along

the length of the dam. The bomb aimer in the nose, Sergeant Johnson, was not satisfied and called off the drop as Joe McCarthy pulled the aircraft up and over the hill at the other side of the valley. Nine more times over the next half hour McCarthy attacked again and again, but only on the tenth run did Johnson release the bomb. His orders were to bomb from the 'lowest practical height', which Johnson later estimated at just 30 feet. A large explosion was seen, but the dam held. After a short while McCarthy set course for base. Perhaps the others would have more luck? But only one other crew attempted an attack; the others had been shot down. Joe McCarthy was awarded the DSO and George Johnson the DFM for their actions on the raid.

A painting by Mark Postlethwaite showing ED825 moments after dropping its Upkeep on the Sorpe Dam in the early hours of 17th May 1943.

Mark Postlethwaite

THE DAMBUSTERS MOVE ON

617 Squadron received new aircraft and new crews and prepared for the next special attack; on the heavily defended Dortmund – Ems Canal. The idea of bouncing the bombs over land, with a forward spin, was abandoned and conventional bombs from standard Lancasters were used. ED825 was used for training flights.

On November 11th/12th 1943, ED825 went to war again, this time as part of a ten strong force to the Antheor Viaduct in southern France. By now it had been re-coded 'AJ-E', and the bomb was a more conventional 12,000lb bomb. The pilot of ED825 on this occasion was Flight Lieutenant O'Shaughnessy who bombed from 8,000 feet on his third run. The results were not as good as expected, with only one direct hit on the viaduct. After bombing, the squadron flew on to North Africa to refuel before making the return flight to England.

23 year old Canadian Gordon Weeden at the controls of his Lancaster.

In December 1943, 617 Squadron received a request for help in dropping supplies to the underground forces in France. The squadrons usually given this sort of work were 138 and 161 based at RAF Tempsford, who flew a mixture of aircraft for dropping supplies and agents into France and other places. On December 8th, four crews were detailed to fly to Tempsford, but this was postponed due to the weather. The weather cleared the next day, so McCarthy (who had flown ED825 on the dams raid), Flight Lieutenant Clayton, Flying Officer Weeden (in ED825) and Warrant Officer Bull took ten ground crew to Tempsford to prepare for the drop the following night.

Flying Officer Gordon Weeden was a Canadian, 23 years old, from Paisley in Ontario. He had with him two other men from the RCAF, but they were both in fact American. Warrant Officer Edward Walters, the 26 year-old bomb aimer, came from Oakmont, Pennsylvania, and the rear gunner,

Above: ED825 as she would have appeared on the night of the Dams raid.

Below L-R;
Gordon Weeden
Edward Walters
Ralph Jones
Robert Howell
Robert Cummings

Warrant Officer Robert Cummings was from Punxsutawney, also in Pennsylvania. The rest of the crew were all RAF:- Sergeant Arthur Richardson, the flight engineer (19) from Enfield in Middlesex; Pilot Officer Ralph Jones, the navigator (22) from Wood Green in Middlesex; Flight Sergeant Robert Howell, the wireless operator (22) from Chingford in Essex; and Sergeant Brook Robinson, the front gunner from Blackley in Manchester. Robinson was the only married man in the crew and, at 31, also well above the average age for aircrew.

ED825 and the seven men took off from RAF Tempsford on December 10th 1943 at 20.35 hours, bound for Doullens in France, on what would probably have seemed an 'easy' trip. Unlike a normal bombing raid to the heart of Germany, fighters and Flak were not predicted, especially flying at low level, and the trip was expected to be relatively short. Crossing the French coast around 21.30 hours they turned south for Doullens; they were never seen again.

TV documentary maker James Cutler, a veteran of 'Fighter Dig Live' had for some years wanted to make a documentary about the Dambusters. He had already interviewed many of those involved in the raid and 617 Squadron, including George 'Johnny' Johnson who had been the bomb aimer in ED825 when it bombed the Sorpe Dam. James Cutler's aim was take 'Johnny' to find 'his' old aircraft, but where was it?

Unlike the other Lancasters that took part in the Dams Raid there was no accurate location given for the crash site of ED825 in published works, or available official archives. The aircraft that had carried Johnny to the Sorpe Dam was lost in the confusion of war and missing records; the task was to positively identify the crash

LIST OF TYPE 464 'DAMBUSTER' LANCASTERS

SERIAL	FATE
ED765	* Prototype. Crashed practicing at Ashley Walk Ranges, 5/8/43
ED817	* Prototype. Scrapped after the war
ED825	Lost over France, 10-11 December 1943
ED864	Crashed on the raid at Marbeck, Germany
ED865	Crashed on the raid at Gilze-Rijen, Holland
ED886	Crashed at Terresmesnil, France, 10-11 December 1943
ED887	Crashed on the raid at Castricum, Holland
ED906	Scrapped after the war
ED909	Scrapped after the war
ED910	Crashed on the raid at Hamm
ED912	Scrapped after the war
ED915	* Failed to take off for the raid. Scrapped after the war
ED918	Crashed at Snettisham, Norfolk, 20/1/44
ED921	Scrapped after the war
ED924	Scrapped after the war
ED925	Crashed on the raid at Ostönnen, Germany
ED927	Crashed on the raid at Rees, Germany
ED929	Scrapped after the war
ED932	Scrapped after the war
ED933	* Scrapped after the war
ED934	Crashed on the raid into the sea off Texel, Holland
ED936	Scrapped in 1944
ED937	Crashed on the raid at Klein Netterden, Germany

* Did not take part in the Dams Raid.

site and, perhaps, to find something that would confirm it as the site of ED825. The production company gave task of locating the crash site to historian Simon Parry, who has specialised in locating many aircraft sites in Britain and Europe. The clues available as a starting point were, at the best, vague. The only concrete evidence lay in the burial site of six of ED825's crew at the tiny village cemetery of Meharicourt, some 20 kilometres east of Amiens. It was common practice for Allied aircrew to be interred in a cemetery close to their place of death, and it was therefore a reasonable assumption that ED825 had fallen within a few kilometres of the village. The pilot's nephew, Gordon Weeden Jnr, had visited Meharicourt in the 1970s and made enquiries as to the location of his uncle's Lancaster, but no one could help and the trail went cold. Very few French or German documents survive that detail Allied losses. Frustratingly a listing in the form of a index to more detailed German reports held in America does not make reference to a Lancaster lost on 10th December 1943.

When the campaign to locate ED825 began in earnest there had been a major development; local historians had begun to take a serious interest in the events of World War Two. People were actively searching for and recording the crash sites of aircraft, like farmer Pierre Ben was who was now seeking wrecks in the region of the Somme, where ED825 was last heard of. Did Pierre know of any sites that could be the missing Dambuster?

Pierre had indeed been told of a Lancaster crash that could well be ED825, but it was 30 kilometres north of Amiens and around 50 kilometres from where its crew

Historian Simon Parry (right) who was given the task of finding ED825, talks to 'Johnny' Johnson who last flew in the aircraft in May 1943.

lay in Meharicourt. The location had been pointed out to author and researcher Jean-Pierre Ducellier, a retired doctor, several years before by Monsieur Tempez who ran a farm with his two sons. By the time Simon arranged the first research visit to Doullens, Monsieur Tempez had passed away, but Dr Ducellier had taken meticulous notes and even had a war-time RAF reconnaissance photograph of the farm showing a disturbed area of ground where the Lancaster had fallen. Monsieur Tempez had told of how the Germans ordered him to move the larger parts of the wreck down a hill to his farm, where they could be loaded onto lorries and taken away. The fields that December were so muddy that the German lorries could not get to the crash site, so he had dragged the parts away with a team of horses.

After several hours searching the area in the photograph not a fragment of aircraft could be found. Something was amiss, for 22 tons of Lancaster wreckage must have left some trace. The story was so convincing that it must have had a basis in fact. Only one final clue remained, a second-hand account that the aircraft had been, 'near the cross'. The cross, it transpired, was the Calvaire Foch, high of the hill overlooking the town; several fields and nearly a kilometre away from the believed location. In a last-ditch effort it was decided to walk from the farm, where the wreck had been dragged to, up the hill towards the cross; swinging metal detectors wearily to-and-fro in the desperate hope of picking up the trail of wreckage. As the sun set over Doullens, the first small piece of aluminium appeared from the earth. But was it ED825?

Gareth Jones with one of the first items of the Lancaster found 'near the cross' as the sun set.

PUTTING THE PIECES TOGETHER

Until the research for this project began very little was known of the last flight of ED825 and its crew. From the interpretation of the finds, the crash site and eye witnesses it has been possible to construct a detailed account of ED825's last moments.

There is no record of any form of loading manifest for ED825 at Tempsford, but it had been loaded with containers carrying weapons. Among the finds at the crash site were rounds of small calibre pistol and machinegun ammunition, including parts of Sten gun magazines. Several 'Mills Bomb' hand grenades were found and reported to the French authorities for disposal. This would suggest that the containers were of the 'H' type containing a mixture of ammunition and explosives. So why would a specially modified 'secret' Lancaster be used for a routine supply drop? Although it can only be speculated as to why crews of 617 Squadron were picked for these supply drops, the Lancasters were no longer as secret as they had been for the Dams Raid. ED825 had been re-fitted with a mid-upper turret, the evidence for this being the 'Taboo follower' found among the wreckage, and almost certainly returned to a more standard configuration. Prior to this project it had been assumed that all the Type 464 'Dambuster' Lancasters had been kept in reserve for future 'Upkeep' operations.

A rare photo of Warrant Officer Bull and his crew, also shot down over Doullens on that night.

As the aircraft approached the town of Doullens it was hit by anti-aircraft fire from a mobile Flak battery mounted on railway carriages in the sidings to the north of the town. Lancaster ED886 AJ-O 'Orange' flown by Warrant Officer Bull was also hit by the anti-aircraft guns, leading to speculation that the operation had been betrayed to the Germans, but there is nothing other than conjecture to substantiate this. Bull was able to make some height and five of his crew were able to parachute to safety before it crashed at Terramesnil - five kilometres south-east of Doullens. ED825 was immediately set afire, probably in its wing fuel tanks, and was described by the only first-hand witness as a 'ball of fire'. From the distance covered between the railway yard and the crash site it can be estimated that the aircraft only stayed in the air for around 35 seconds after it was hit. The burning aircraft flew over the town from west to east, in the l'Authie valley, before it turned to starboard and flew into the rising ground east of the ruelle Merlin. In the seconds after the aircraft was hit the rear gunner, Warrant Officer Robert Cummings, attempted to escape. He opened the doors of his turret into the fuselage where his parachute was stored and then made his way to the rear escape hatch. He pulled the emergency handle on the floor and jettisoned the hatch, but by that time the aircraft was too low for his parachute to open; he died the following day. The other six men were killed in the crash.

The subsequent fire reduced some of the airframe to molten aluminium and exploded the ammunition. The surface wreckage was thoroughly cleared by the Germans with the assistance of Monsieur Tempez, the farmer, and the site was left to grass over of its own accord.

The field has remained in pasture since 1943 and has not been ploughed. Only one small area was identified where parts were found at a depth greater than 0.3 metres, leading to the conclusion that the aircraft had not dived steeply to the ground, but had flown into the gently rising hill close to its summit and burnt on the surface.

The remains of six crew members were removed to Meharicourt for burial, but the body of Robert Cummings is now buried at the Canadian War Cemetery, Leubringhen, near Calais.

The American rear gunner, Robert Cummings, who used the escape hatch and very nearly escaped death.

THE RELATIVES' STORY   GORDON WEEDEN JNR

One Friday in October 2007 I returned to my home in Ontario to find the light on my answer phone flashing. With one press of a button my wife and I were launched on an emotional odyssey that would leave a deep impression on us both. I had been named after my uncle who I knew had been in the air force, as had my father. Gordon had been killed on operations with 617 Squadron over France, that much I knew, but the family had often wanted to know more.

I listened to the message over again;

"My name is James, I am a television producer, I make documentaries. I'm making a film about the plane that Gordon Weeden flew. Unfortunately he lost his life during the crash. I am doing some research on it. I'll try to call you again. If this is of interest to you perhaps you could give me a call; don't worry I can call you, I'll try again perhaps at a more convenient time. Thanks very much." Well?

James called back a couple of hours later and explained the project in more detail. He was shooting a documentary on Lancaster ED825, Gordon's plane, which his team thought they had located in France. At first this seemed a little unreal. I was sceptical of the call and the motive behind the proposal. Was he some kind of Crank? But James continued to provide details that confirmed his depth of knowledge of Gordon and the circumstances surrounding the crash. It still seemed a little unreal, even

Gordon Weeden Jr and his wife Mary on location in Doullens.

though there was excitement on receiving the news. I was interested, but wanted to talk to the family. I also asked James to email a little background on the project and its sponsors. After several emails, much discussion and calling in favours from family members, I told James that my wife and I would come over to France to participate in the excavation of Gordon's plane - one of the best on-the-spot decision we ever made.

My mind was still spinning as my wife and I crossed the Atlantic a few days later. Was this indeed the plane that Gordon was flying? What was his mission, how will it feel at the site? My family was excited that we were going and I wondered what did we want to get from this trip? What would it offer to our family history and would it be worth it?

When we met James and his team for breakfast in the village of Doullens we had no idea what was in store for us. There was excitement around the table, books, drawings and a keen interest in our binder of Gordon's history.

No one could have predicted the range of feelings that I experienced when James took me to the crash site. It was so peaceful, yet the knowledge that I was standing on the soil where Gordon died was overwhelming. The quiet little village of Doullens in the valley below and the rolling countryside contrasted with the violence of war that shot Gordon and his crew from the sky.

Although I knew Gordon had crashed in France, it was important to me to know exactly where and under what circumstances. As I participated in the dig and evidence of the crash was uncovered I was impressed by the knowledge of the team and their passion for what they were finding. Each time I was offered the opportunity to touch a piece of the aircraft there were flashes of pride, sadness and thankfulness for what men like Gordon had done for us. I wish I had been able to share this experience with Gordon's father and his brother; my Father.

I had visited the graves of Gordon and his crew in 1969, but on this visit the emotions were more intense. Not only had I now found the crash site, but I had new information about the plane and the crash.

It was also important, and emotional, to meet Johnny Johnson, the bomb aimer in ED825. Johnny represented the era of the war and afforded a connection with an uncle that I never knew.

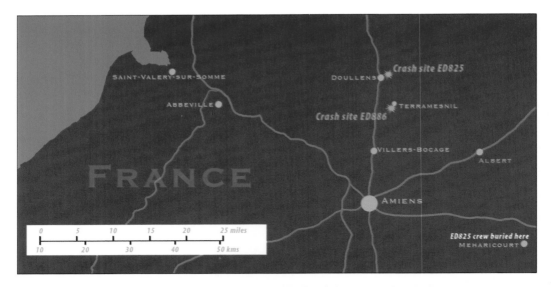

THE EXCAVATION

On the strength of a few shreds of evidence and a hand-full of tiny fragments the dig was 'on'. The 'History Channel UK' was backing what was now a major event. The 'Daily Mirror' was sending a team, Cy and his crew of Atypical Media set up base camp and the Weedens were on their way from Canada. The Mayor and the townspeople of Doullens had prepared a reception,

the Tempez brothers had moved the cows and we were about to bring Johnny and his family to a wind-swept French hillside for the weekend!

With an event such as this there was no possibility of a trial excavation to reassure ourselves of what was there; Cy wanted to catch the moment of discovery - to give it some 'edge'.

The area where the metal detectors had indicated the concentration of pieces to lay was marked out and the team quickly began to find parts scattered far and wide. It became clear from the shallow depth of the finds that ED825 had not dived steeply into the ground, but had flown into the rising ground and burnt. Exploded rounds of machine-gun ammunition from the turrets showed how the fire had spread and small pools of once molten aluminium gave an indication of the fire's

Gordon Weeden Jnr at the Meharicourt cemetery, confusingly some 50 kilometres from the crash site.

94

Amongst the first finds were this ammunition box lock from the nose turret (above) and more importantly, rounds of 9mm pistol ammunition (right) which could only have come from the container being dropped to the Resistance on that night.
(A normal .303 round is shown for comparison).

ferocity. Tellingly, small components from the nose turret were confined to a small area where the nose of the bomber had come to rest on one edge of the debris field. The location of the nose in relation to the other parts indicated the likely flight-path of ED825 in its last moments. By the end of the first day a small area to the north-east of the main site was producing some strange finds, pistol ammunition and pieces of wood. As darkness fell what was thought to be the remains of a container that once held the stores to be dropped to the Resistance appeared. The idea that we were excavating a container fitted what we were finding very nicely; circular, mostly made of wood and about the diameter of dustbin.

Fired by the hope that something might be found to confirm that this was ED825 the activity on the second morning focused on the container and its stores. There was mounting evidence of the supplies that never reached the Resistance and the wooden framework of the container was carefully lifted from its hole. Heads were scratched to interpret what we had now that pieces of Perspex were found attached to it, an inspection port perhaps? It was Alex Bateman, the Dambuster authority, who excitedly put forward his theory and dashed off to fetch a portfolio of Avro

Above: The dig went on into the darkness as the team examined the strange finds to the north-east of the main site.

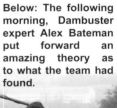

Below: The following morning, Dambuster expert Alex Bateman put forward an amazing theory as to what the team had found.

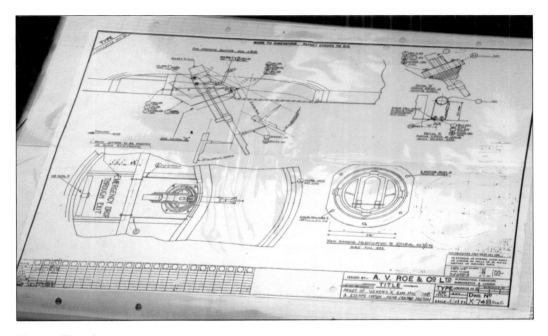

Above: The Avro drawings of the lower gun position and (below) the small triangular mount is clearly visible under the fuselage of ED825.

works drawings that showed adaptions made to ED825. As he spread the drawings out and orientated the pieces of wood, Perspex and aluminium it became clear that we had found something unique to the Type 464 Provisioning Lancasters – the lower gun mounting.

THE LOWER GUN POSITION

The Lancasters used on the Dambuster Raid differed in many ways from the standard bomber, but the most noticeable change was the removal of the mid-upper turret. To compensate for the loss of firepower it was proposed that a machine-gun be installed aft of the bomb-bay with a single Vickers Gas Operated (VGO) drum fed gun pointing below that tail. The first three modified Lancasters were fitted with the gunner's position, but only ED825 had the gun fitted and it was sent for firing trials at A&AEE Boscome Down. The gun position also doubled as an escape hatch and the 'lower gunner' would crouch by the circular hatch, peering through the Perspex, but it was soon decided to abandon the idea as it was 'useless'. During ED825's time at Boscome Down a series of photographs were taken that became a standard reference for 'Dambuster' Lancasters, the lower gun can clearly be seen on the photographs and led to the assumption that all the aircraft were thus modified – which is why thousands of plastic model Dambusters around the world sport a lower gun!

Although the gun was of no practical use the 'escape hatch' was left in place, probably with the empty magnesium alloy ball mount.

Although no drawings survive to show the mounting for the rear downward facing spotlight it seems likely that this gun mount was altered on subsequent aircraft with either the aft facing hole for the gun covered and a new one cut which faced forward, or the mounting reworked on the line and fitted facing forward. ED825 did not have lights on the Dambuster Raid, one reason possibly because it still had the gun mount in place and there was not enough time to reconstruct the whole thing. As no lights were fitted for the Sorpe attack or after, it remained with the gun mount in place until it was lost. We had just found the world's only Dambuster hatch and gun mount – and discovered that it was constructed slightly differently to the Avro specification.

As details of the finds were recorded it was clear that the hatch / gun position was unusually intact and undamaged in comparison with the rest of the items. It is therefore quite feasible that the hatch had been found some distance from the main wreck and was dumped into a convenient hole during the cleanup operations,

Alex Bateman (right) explains the gun position to Mark Postlethwaite.

thus escaping the impact and fire that had so comprehensively destroyed the rest of the plane. Eventually a theory that would explain this was formulated and this also added a sad footnote to the crew's final moments. An emergency release handle was incorporated in the hatch, which released two pins that allowed the whole hatch to fall away and provide an emergency exit. The American born rear gunner, Warrant Officer Robert Cummings, may well have come forward from his turret to release the hatch and attempted to escape through it. It was subsequently learnt that he fell some 300 metres from the bomber's impact point and it is recorded that he died the following day.

THE TABOO FOLLOWER MYSTERY

The final area to be investigated was the steep embankment to the north-east of the main impact point. It was thought likely that some parts of the aircraft may have been unceremoniously dumped over the fence by the farmer as he tried to tidy up his field. Certainly there was all manner of modern rubbish, so a scramble down the bank was worth a try. A mixture of small parts proved the theory correct, but one small part held great significance. Ian Hodgkiss picked up a short length of 'H' section aluminium with a funny little rubber wheel on the end, *"That's from the Taboo Rail"* he declared. Heaven knows in what dark corner of his memory the information was stored, but the part was just visible on some photos of mid-upper

Left; Ian Hodgkiss (left) searching the embankment where the Taboo Follower was found.
Above left; Some of the excavation team sift through the fragments.

turrets – the trouble was the Dambuster Lancasters did not have that turret! Two of the curious little wheels protruded from below the guns on the turret and ran on a curved rail on the fuselage that lifted the wheels up when the gunner was in danger of shooting off the tail of his own aircraft. The only explanation for this find was that ED825 had been fitted with a mid-upper turret after the Dams Raid and this had gone unrecorded.

The Lancasters that survived the raid were kept at readiness until the end of the war should another use be found for the remaining Upkeep bouncing bombs. The aircraft were kept under guard as they were still regarded as 'Top Secret', but why would 'secret' aircraft be used on risky, but routine, supply dropping missions over France where they could fall into enemy hands? This had led to speculation that at least some of the equipment had been removed from some of the bombers. The finding of this small component confirmed that some Type 464 Provisioning Lancasters had indeed been wholly or partially converted back to a standard bomber configuration, a fact not previously known.

Above: This close up of the mid-upper turret of a standard Lancaster clearly shows the two taboo wheels protruding from the front of the turret. (The guns are not fitted on this training flight).

Left: The remains of one of ED825's taboo wheels, proving that it had been refitted with a mid-upper turret after the Dams raid.

RUMOUR OF BETRAYAL

Two Lancasters had flown over the town of Doullens just before midnight on December 10th, 1943 and both were brought down by Flak coming from guns mounted on trains in the sidings. Was this a quirk of fate, or was there more to it? A rumour persists that far from it being a freak event, an informer within the Resistance network had informed the Germans that a supply drop was planned. For the supply drop to be effective the resistance workers had to set out a pattern of lights in a remote area where the signal would not be seen by the Germans at a time and location known by the SOE in London and briefed to the bomber crews. By late 1943, however, German intelligence had infiltrated the resistance network in the Amiens / Doullens area and was rapidly breaking down the organisation. Whether news of the supply drop was leaked to the Germans, or whether the Flak train pulled into Doullens by chance that night can never be proved one way or the other.

THE SUPPLY DROP – PART OF A GREATER PLAN

One of the hand-grenades from the supply cannister being carried by ED825.

The area of the Somme was a particularly important part of France at that period of the war for Allied planners. Although only the most senior of Allied officers knew it at that time, it was less than six months before the planned D-Day invasion. The Allies tried everything to deceive the Germans and convince them that the landing would NOT be in Normandy. The idea was to convince the Germans that the attack would be in the north of France; Pas de Calais or Somme Estuary. Part of the extraordinarily convoluted plan called for British intelligence in London to start making lots of noise in the area – building up the Resistance, putting in agents and dropping supplies, which was what ED825 and her crew had been doing. The Germans saw what was happening and took the bait. The deception, code name Operation Fortitude South, worked; even after D-Day the Germans held back reinforcements, waiting for the 'real' landings in Somme Estuary which gave the Allies time to establish a bridgehead in Normandy before the Panzers moved south.

JOHNNY'S JOURNEY

The producers had arranged for 'Johnny' Johnson who flew in ED825 on the Dams Raid to attend the dig in Doullens to provide a tangible link to the past. 'Johnny' who was in his late 80s was not well enough to fly and so had to make the long journey from Torquay by car, accompanied by his son and grandsons.

With the people of Doullens wanting to honour Johnny with a special service of remembrance near the crash site followed by a civic ceremony and lunch, the veteran Dambuster was faced

with a gruelling schedule apart from his filming commitments. A large group of French veterans and dignitaries assembled at the Calvaire Foch for a wreath laying ceremony in which Johnny laid a wreath in memory of the crew of ED825 who died in the crash. The entire group then drove down into the town for the civic reception where speeches were made and gifts were exchanged between the English, French and Canadian representatives.

George 'Johnny' Johnson interviewed by French television reporters at Doullens.

The town of Doullens honours the men who gave their lives dropping supplies to the Resistance.

The Mayor of Doullens, with Johnny and Gordon Weeden Jnr.

Johnny was asked to talk through his attack on the Sorpe Dam with the aid of a model Lancaster - and a very roughly constructed dam!

In the late afternoon, after the ceremonial dinner, Johnny was finally driven to the crash site itself. Despite the long tiring day he had endured, Johnny threw himself into the planned filming with the gusto of a man half his age. After filming some scenes with the pieces found so far, Johnny was asked to talk through his attack on the Sorpe Dam with the aid of a model Lancaster and a very roughly constructed dam, built by the team earlier in the day. With night having fallen the filming lights were illuminated, the diggers stood back and Johnny 'took to the stage'. What followed was a unique retelling of the attack on the Sorpe Dam by a man who was there and remembered every last detail. It was a privilege for all the crew to witness it and a spontaneous round of applause echoed around that cold misty hillside that night when it was over.

After a dinner in the evening with all the team, Johnny was led to bed much against his wishes but in anticipation of his early start the following morning. At first light, Johnny and Gordon Weeden were driven to Meharicourt to film at the graves of Gordon's uncle and the crew of ED825. After this

Two generations pay their respects at Meharicourt.

Johnny holds the souvenir Perspex!

100km round trip it was back to the crash site for more filming. The final scenes were for the team to show Johnny the most interesting finds and get his reaction to seeing them again after all those years. One of the digging team had found an exceptionally large piece of Perspex which he had spent all night cleaning in the hope that Johnny would sign it as a personal memento of the day. As the team handed these items to Johnny for his comments, he was captivated by this piece as it was most likely from the bomb-aimer's blister which of course he last looked through on the night of the Dams raid. He immediately thanked the team for presenting him with such a lovely memento and as he walked back to the car the team cast worried glances at the unfortunate digger whose entire night's work was now on its way back to Torquay!

A NORFOLK TRAGEDY

'REEDHAM MARSH'

TIME TEAM

CHANNEL 4

FIRST SHOWN: FEBRUARY 1999

DIRECTOR: SIMON RAIKES

PRODUCTION COMPANY: VIDEOTEXT / PICTURE HOUSE

A NORFOLK TRAGEDY

The iconic American bomber of WW2 was the Boeing B-17 'Flying Fortress' which, with the less charismatic B24 'Liberator', populated the skies over Norfolk and Suffolk in 1944 and 1945.

Astonishingly 7,775 B-17s came to the flat fenlands, 2,577 were lost on operations and many others in accidents. 47,000 American airmen lost their lives while serving with the US 8th Air Force based in England.

Formations of B-17s such as this were a regular sight in the skies over Norfolk during the war.

1964

By the 1960s the deserted runways and abandoned buildings of the many old airfields scattered across Norfolk and Suffolk stood as the only reminder to the US 8th Air Force, but many locals were keen to learn what had happened there. One such young man was 16 year-old Ian McLachlan, in 1964 a Cadet Sergeant in the Air Training Corps. Although barely 20 years had passed since war had ravaged the skies over the marshes, the details of events there had already slipped into legend and half-truths – like the tale of a German bomber still buried in Reedham Marsh! Before long a party of ATC cadets persuaded a local to take them across the marshes to where he knew the aircraft to have fallen; but it was not German, it was an American bomber and not one but two – lost in a collision.

The guide led the cadets to a small pond in the marsh, close to Mill Dyke, and around the pond were scattered parts of a war-time bomber – exciting things indeed for an air-minded teenager. Among the reeds was an oxygen bottle and part of a fuel tank, but nothing that could identify the aircraft. A quarter of a mile across the marsh was Decoy Carr, where the second aircraft had fallen, but there was nothing to be found there. The lure of bomber parts was great indeed for the boys. In the bleak, frozen, days of January 1964 several visits were made to delve chilled hands into the murky pond until eventually a clue appeared; a part with the name 'Boeing' stamped on it. It was a B-17!

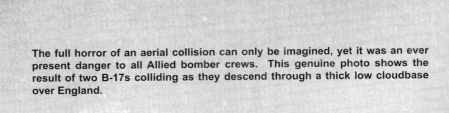

The full horror of an aerial collision can only be imagined, yet it was an ever present danger to all Allied bomber crews. This genuine photo shows the result of two B-17s colliding as they descend through a thick low cloudbase over England.

The Norfolk Constabulary turned up a mention of planes crashing at Reedham Marsh on 21st February 1944, barely twenty years earlier. The bombers had collided coming back from a raid and all the airmen had been killed. Ian was hooked. Over the next year more information was forthcoming and the two B-17s were identified, but which had fallen at Mill Dyke and which at Decoy Carr could not be established. By 1965 the enthusiasm of the cadets had waned, leaving only Ian and his friend Paul to carry on with the quest. More parts were pulled from the pond; oxygen masks, a parachute, and occasionally fuel bubbled to the surface to leave its rainbow film on the surface. Finally, a panel was found bearing the number 42-31370 – the mystery had been solved. The aircraft and men involved had been identified:

Captain John N Hutchison and his crew.

Mill Dyke
B-17G 42-31370
550th Squadron, 385th Bomb Group

Captain John N Hutchison (pilot)
2/Lt Charles G Curtis (co-pilot)
1/Lt John E Epps (navigator)
1/Lt Edmond J Gamble (bombardier)
Tech Sgt Roy C Kitner (top gunner)
Staff Sgt Joseph J Carpinetti (tail gunner)
Tech Sgt William J Dukes (radio operator)
Staff Sgt John H Erhardt (ball gunner)
Staff Sgt Emilio Corgnatti (left waist gunner)
Staff Sgt Peter Bobulsky Jr. (right waist gunner)
Staff Sgt Frank L Creegan Jr. (photographer)

Decoy Carr
B-17 42-37963
549th Squadron, 385th Bomb Group

1/Lt Warren J Pease
2/Lt Edward B Brown (co-pilot)
2/Lt Bernard Kaplan (navigator)
2/Lt Robert E Jenkins (bombardier)
Tech Sgt William R Clift (top gunner)
Staff Sgt Junior M Falls (tail gunner)
Tech Sgt William Gill Jr. (radio operator)
Staff Sgt Franklin C Owsley (ball gunner)
Staff Sgt Harold E Dickason (left waist gunner)
Staff Sgt Gail F Bruner (right waist gunner)

Lieutenant Warren J Pease.

B-17s of the 385th Bomb Group leave heavy contrails as they head for their target in 1944.

MONDAY 21ST FEBRUARY 1944

Captain John Hutchison and his crew clambered to their posts at Great Ashfield. Their aircraft was simply known as '370', a replacement for their regular B-17 the faithful 'Sleepytime Gal' that had seen them safely through most of their 24 missions. This was to be the 25th and final mission of their tour, after which they could join the 'Lucky Bastard's Club' and return stateside to take up 'safe' jobs as instructors. The target was Diepholz, an aircraft depot in north-western Germany and considered an easy trip compared to Schweinfurt, Regensburg and the other targets upon which so many crews had been lost. Joining them for the final mission was Sergeant Frank L 'Bud' Creegan, a photographer to record the great day.

Of the thirty-four B-17s of the 385th Bomb Group that set out for Diepholz only one was lost; hit by Flak it was seen fall behind the formation and was left behind. As they crossed the Norfolk coast on their return celebrations began in Hutchison's plane. Below them stretched a layer of cloud as far as the eye could see, completely obscuring the land below. Hutchison, being an experienced captain, led a formation of three B-17s down towards the cloud; on his right wing was Warren Pease and to his left John Terrace. The three bomber pilots gently lowered themselves into the all enveloping cloud, relying solely on the panel of instruments to stay level and on course. Some minutes later and 3,000 feet lower Hutchison came out from below the cloud and saw John Terrace on his left, just where he should have been, but there was no sign of Warren Pease.

Terrace's crew looked across and later recalled seeing Hutchison smoking a large cigar – lucky bastards indeed! As the crew looked on enviously another B-17 dived steeply out from the cloud behind them, passed below both aircraft, and then reared up in front of Hutchison's B-17. It was the missing aircraft of Warren Pease. The two aircraft collided, right in front of the disbelieving eyes of John Terrace and his crew. The tail section and rear gun position of Pease's maverick bomber were torn off by the propellers of Hutchison's starboard inner engine. For a moment Warren Pease's B-17 hung in the air – them tumbled onto its back – and fell on top of Hutchison's aircraft, cutting its fuselage in two.

Only the rear gunner and Bob Goldsmith, who was looking out from the waist position, of John Terrace's aircraft witnessed the full horror as two men were thrown out of the bombers without parachutes. The wreckage of the two bombers fell the last 1,000 feet to earth and exploded in two fire-balls. Twenty-one men had died just minutes from safety.

1976

Having established the identities of two bombers on Reedham Marsh, Ian McLachlan let things rest for ten years. A parachute that he had discovered in the pond formed by Hutchison's B-17 was donated to the USAAF Museum in Ohio and is now kept in a sealed case; seen by nearly 200,000 visitors each year.

A new group of enthusiasts assembled at the crash site of Warren Pease's B-17 in 1976. 32 years had now passed since the crash and interest in the history of World War 2 and the air war over East Anglia had

Ian McLachlan with one of the Wright Cyclone engines.

developed, leading to the establishment of small museums and aircraft recovery groups. A JCB was brought to the site at Decoy Carr and soon pulled an assortment of wreckage and a complete three-bladed propeller from the ground. A machine gun and navigator's instruments followed, but then the JCB's bucket caught on something so large that it defeated the driver's attempts to raise it to the surface. The JCB slid into marsh and had, itself, to be rescued. The project was abandoned.

Two years later, in 1978, a much larger digger was brought to the crash site of John Hutchison's aircraft. From the same pond that Ian had pulled the first parts out of 22 years earlier there appeared a mass of wreckage and finally one of the

Propeller blades are lifted from the crash site of Hutchison's B-17.

mighty Wright Cyclone engines. The engine, propellers and many other items recovered over the past two decades were donated to local aviation museums to act as testimony to the sacrifices of American airmen in East Anglia.

ENTER TIME TEAM

The poignancy and tragedy of the disaster at Reedham Marsh never deserted Ian McLachlan, who established himself as a leading aviation historian and author. In 1998, thirty-four years after his first visit to Reedham Marsh, Ian found himself back there and in front of the 'TimeTeam' cameras. Planning for the dig had taken over a year, during which time Ian's original proposal to excavate both aircraft had been rejected in favour of an excavation of the B-17 flown by Warren Pease – because it had been less well excavated. The land around Reedham in the Norfolk Broads is crisscrossed by a network of ditches and dykes that drain the land for cultivation. The fragile 'crust' of topsoil 'floats' on a bed of soft peat and clay and the area is now listed as an SSSI – Site of Special Scientific Interest. This posed a new set of problems for the production company which had to gain the agreement of many environmental authorities and organizations. The prime areas of concern were that the excavation would change the hydrochemistry of the dyke waters and

damage the dyke walls. It was agreed that water from the dyke would be pumped 400 metres to a water-storage lagoon with oil absorption booms that would filter the water before returning it to the dyke – a hugely expensive operation.

The scale and complexity of the operation to recover the B-17 flown by Warren Pease can be judged from this view of the excavation at Decoy Carr.

Director Simon Raikes was in charge when filming began in June 1998. In addition to the regular Time Team members and crew there were representatives from several East Anglian aircraft recovery groups, an RAF bomb disposal team, the St John Ambulance, retired air crash investigator Bernie Forward and assorted other experts.

After Tony Robinson had filmed his traditional 'just three days' piece to camera the excavation began. This was the first aircraft excavation that the regular 'Time Team' members had undertaken and it was not long before differences of opinion between the archaeologists and 'aircraft-diggers' began to surface. After thirty-four years Ian finally had the tools at hand to complete a thorough excavation of Warren Pease's B-17 – two tracked Hymacs – but progress was, as Ian put it, 'painfully slow'. As the two Hymacs and their drivers stood idle Phil Harding took over 'Trench One' with his trowel. He had uncovered the top of a massive screw-jack from the main undercarriage and began to carefully grid and draw his find in time-honoured fashion, but already it was becoming clear that the hoped for wreckage would never be reached in this way. A few small parts were found in other areas around the site, including a condom! A sequence where Ian explained to Carenza the use of a condom - to protect gun barrels from dust and moisture – was filmed, but not used.

Phil Harding from TimeTeam records some of the early finds.

One of the machine guns emerges from the mud.

On the second day the Hymac replaced the trowel, but before long the depth and safety of the excavation was being called into question. Now halfway through the excavation they had still not reached the heavy wreckage the JCB had hit twenty-two years before! Frustrated that he might never discover what lay beyond the original excavation Ian McLachlan suggested to the head-man, series producer Tim Taylor, that the pace should be picked up. Seizing the chance of good TV moment, Tim staged a 'strong, on camera debate' between the regular team and Ian that highlighted the differences in the two opposing approaches. Methodical archaeology was all very well, but recovering several tons of war-time bomber was a different matter! The reason being that the date was already known and any archaeological context was diminished to almost nothing by previous recovery efforts, including those to extricate the crew.

On the third and final day caution was thrown to the winds and the Hymac drivers had their day. Plunging digger buckets ever deeper into the marsh and dyke wreckage surfaced from ever deeper in 'Trench One'; armoured glass from the windscreen and two machine guns. Finally, it had to be admitted by all that they had found all that remained of the B-17 and the excavation would have to be closed down.

In a final sequence Tony Robinson appeared on the back of a restored American truck carrying the propeller blades and other wreckage from the 1976 dig. They had been on site from the beginning and everyone knew their background, but when the programme was finally shown the impression was given that they had 'just been discovered' - this being far from the case! Air crash investigator Bernie Forward cast an experienced eye over the propellers and immediately noticed something amiss – the blades on one had been 'feathered' before the crash. A propeller would normally only be feathered if an engine had failed, when the blades would be turned 'edge on' to the airflow to minimize the drag. From this discovery a theory was developed that gave a possible cause of the accident. Bernie proposed that an engine on Warren Pease's B-17 had failed whilst descending through the cloud and during the process of feathering the propeller the aircraft had entered a dive. When he appeared from the cloud Pease pulled up steeply to avoid hitting the ground and climbed into the path of John Hutchison, thus causing the collision.

The .5 Browning machine guns and other wreckage arranged in front of the 'nose art' painted by Anne Haywood who painted many of the war-time bombers.

Filming one of the last scenes, when the propeller blades appear on a restored war-time Diamond T truck.

There was no doubt that less wreckage had been found than had been hoped for, but Bernie had plausibly solved the mystery of why the two bombers had collided. 'Reedham Marsh' was first shown on 21st February 1999, fifty-five years, to the very day, after the crash. Controversial though the programme was, it stirred many and varied emotions and had the highest viewing figures of any previous TimeTeam episode.

BACK TO MILL DYKE

In September 1999 a final attempt to excavate the Hutchison's B-17 was made. Freed of the constraints of television, veteran digger driver Vic Doughty took his ditching Hymac to Mill Dyke. Vic had driven the machines on earlier digs and for Time Team the year before, now he thought he knew where more wreckage lay. Conditions here were better than at Decoy Carr, the ground was firmer and the hole did not flood. Wreckage appeared again and, at a depth of 5 metres, an engine appeared – with its propeller still attached. A second propeller followed and more twisted and burnt panels and components that once constituted a 'Flying Fortress'. As the excavation drew to a close Ian's son discovered a camera – the K-20 used by photographer Bud Creegan who had gone along to record Hutchison's 25th and final mission. The camera did not look too badly damaged and had been sealed

from daylight in the earth; was it just possible that a last ghostly image of the lost crew had survived? Photographic experts at the Imperial War Museum's Duxford facility took Bud Creegan's camera into their darkroom and examined it under infrared light, but found only one badly damaged piece of film – the back of the camera and the film cassette had been ripped away in the crash and the last pictures of Hutchison's crew lost.

The camera - sadly too badly damaged for its film to have survived.

After 36 years Ian McLachan finally drew his project to a close when a memorial to the twenty-one young men who had been killed on the marshes was unveiled in Reedham Village. The marble plaque is positioned next to the village's tribute to their own fallen of both wars, honouring the 47,000 airmen from America who gave their lives flying from Britain.

SUNKEN INVADERS

'BOMBERS IN THE MARSH'
TIME TEAM

CHANNEL 4

FIRST SHOWN: JANUARY 2005

DIRECTOR: SIMON RAIKES

PRODUCTION COMPANY: VIDEOTEXT / PICTURE HOUSE

SUNKEN INVADERS

In 2004 the TimeTeam production team had been looking for another aircraft excavation project. The B-17 at Reedham Marsh had ultimately proved disappointing and the Spitfire in France had been voted one of the top ten programmes; but each had produced only shattered components, not a recognisable aircraft. The criteria for the 'ideal' excavation were that the remains must be 'recognisable' as an aircraft and there must be the usual 'mystery' to solve. A pretty tall order for a crash site in the UK, as such sites are more associated with remote jungles or inaccessible mountain peaks.

The Lancashire Aircraft Investigation Team headed by Nick Wotherspoon stepped forward to meet the challenge with a proposal to excavated not one, but two bombers that had crashed in river estuary mud - nearly a mile from solid ground!

The aim was to excavate the crash sites of two A-26 Invader aircraft that had collided shortly after take-off over the marshes close to the then American airbase at Warton. This project was the culmination of months of planning and preparation as the site was probably one of the most demanding that the LAIT, or the TimeTeam had ever attempted to work on.

From photographs of the crash scene taken in 1944 it was possible to gain a rough idea of where the remains of the two aircraft should lie in relation to each other, but not exactly where the wrecks now lay. Work also began on tracking down any surviving witnesses or relatives of the crews.

The A-26 Invader was a sleek and heavily armed aircraft, which entered service with the USAAF in early summer 1944.

The aircraft involved were two A-26B Invaders; 43-22298 and 43-22336. Both had been built at the Douglas plant at Tulsa, Oklahoma and flown to the UK. Production records indicate that the two aircraft differed slightly - a factor that would prove important 60 years later. The aircraft were then transferred to the American, Base Air Depot 2 (BAD2) at Warton where they joined others awaiting allocation to front line units of the Ninth Air Force, in replacement for A-20 and B-26 aircraft. One of these units was the 641st Squadron of the 409th Bombardment Group who had been based at Station A-48, Bretigny, Seine Oise, France, since September 1944. The squadron flew regular combat sorties, mostly against close support targets, in their A-20s. In mid November the squadron began converting to the A-26 and sent a group of pilots with their old A-20s to Warton to familiarise themselves with the new aircraft. After some training they would fly them directly back to base.

The wreck of 2nd Lt Zuber's plane.

The tail of A-26 43-22298 flown by Lt Hubbard.

As the background research progressed in the months leading up to the dig the events surrounding the accident became clear. Just after midday on 29th November 1944 the A-26s began taking off from BAD2 and got into formation over the airfield, ready for the return flight to France. Some 20 aircraft were seen over the base, where the bombers were forming up in four flights of six aircraft. A-26 Invader 43-22298 was being flown by 2nd Lt. Kenneth E. Hubbard accompanied by Private John F. Guy, a crew chief. Hubbard was taking up his position up as No. 6 in the first flight, when his aircraft collided with another A-26, 43-22336 flown by 2nd Lt. Norman Zuber.

One aircraft seemed to explode as they collided. A fellow pilot from Hubbard's flight saw a ball of flame with a propeller protruding from it as it fell. He was so shocked that he continued the flight out of formation, keeping a safe distance from the other aircraft. The second aircraft fell out of control with one wing missing outboard of the engine. It all happened so fast that the witness statements at the time seem confused as to what had actually occurred.

Both planes fell on tidal mudflats in the Ribble estuary, close to the base at Warton, and at first there seemed hope that there could be survivors. As crowds gathered at the waters edge some thought they saw movement inside one of the fuselages. Many servicemen from BAD2 had witnessed the tragedy and one of them, Sergeant Stanley C. Begonsky, immediately began to wade and then swim out to the burning aircraft. He was the first to reach the crash scene. The fire at the first aircraft had by now died down, but as he looked into the cockpit he realised that the two crewmen inside were beyond help. He then waded to the second plane that was still burning. At first Begonsky could see little through the thick smoke. Crouching down he chopped his way into

**Above:
Lt Kenneth Hubbard.**

Left: 2nd Lt Norman Zuber (centre).

the cockpit where he found the pilot amidst the flames and began to drag him out; sadly he was beyond help. Norman Zuber had been killed instantly.

By this time several lifeboatmen had arrived at the scene in the local lifeboat tender - the lifeboat itself being out of action whilst undergoing repairs. They recovered the two bodies from the first aircraft with the help of Begonsky, who showed them how to gain access to the cockpit. Begonsky then returned amid exploding flares and burning fuel to recover the third body and the lifeboat tender took them all

back to the shore. Sergeant Begonsky and the ten lifeboatmen received awards for gallantry for their rescue attempts.

The wrecks were of little value to the American Air Force and were left where they had fallen, gradually disappearing from view as the marsh began to consolidate and the level of mud rose to cover them. Only the tail of Hubbard's aircraft remained visible by the 1950s, providing occasional shelter during inclement weather for the few hardy wildfowlers who ventured out on to this part of the marsh.

Above and below, The tail of Hubbard's A-26 - seperated by 60 years.

Two members of the Lancashire Aircraft Investigation Team had made an expedition to the site in the 1980s when two propeller blade tips had been visible, but 25 years later these too had apparently vanished beneath the marsh.

The first attempt to locate the wrecks had been abortive, the area was too vast and inaccessible to make a search easy. The next visit was planned for the end of February 2005 after many hours poring over photographs from the crash report and aerial surveys at the local Record Office. The position of the wrecks had been plotted, now would theory translate into practice!

The preparation paid off and both aircraft were pin pointed. Four engines and the two propeller tips were still there, hidden in the grass - discovered by tripping over one of them.

Planning now began in earnest with permit applications being submitted to the MoD and consultation with regards to the equipment and logistics that would be required to carry out an excavation in such difficult terrain. As preparations progressed it became clear that the essential MoD permits were not being granted. The site was designated as a SSSI and a permit could not be issued without first gaining the consent of English Nature - the researchers had been awaiting MoD consent before approaching English Nature!

JUST THREE DAYS

Misunderstanding resolved, preparations for the dig began two days before filming. The famous TimeTeam 'incident room' was set up at the British Aerospace Warton Sports Club. Tracks across the marsh were marked out, tidal gutters bridged and plant moved out to the site. Two Hagglund BV206 all-terrain personnel carriers were used to carry people and equipment to the site. Other specialist equipment included a third, trailer equipped, Hagglund, a six wheeled all-terrain crane-equipped Supacat, two high flotation tracked 20 ton excavators, one with a long-reach arm, and a 12 ton tracked dumper; plenty of toys to play with. Various 'experts' were brought in, including Guy De La Bédoyère and Air Crash Investigator Steve Moss, as well as RAF 'crash and smash' and Ordnance Disposal teams.

A small army had assembled for the first day of filming which would focus on Hubbard's aircraft. Trenches were opened on the tail section of Hubbard's aircraft and one of the four engines. Geophys surveyed the areas of the two crashes, glad that the search areas had been narrowed down from the 20 or so acres months earlier - the fancy wheeled 'pram-like' contraption was unable to cope with the conditions and broke! Progress on the engine in a second trench was rapid with the excavator carefully avoiding the upright propeller blade that had protruded only a couple of inches above the surface. Once the engine was reached the excavation continued by hand. A nearby gutter had been dammed and the excavation stayed surprisingly dry. Unfortunately the same could not be said over at the tail where almost constant ingress of water made conditions very sticky indeed. The engine proved remarkably undamaged and cylinder heads, exhaust stacks and ignition

The tail of Hubbard's A-26 had become entombed in estuary mud.

A second trench was opened to reveal one of the engines from 2nd Lt Norman Zuber's plane.

harness were soon revealed as well as the still attached propeller with all three blades intact. The reduction gear casing, where the engine maker's plate would have been, had corroded away, making identification of it and therefore the plane this engine had originated from, difficult. Fortunately one of the modifications known to have been incorporated on one of the aircraft was the fitting of R-2800-71 engines, with an improved ignition system using the distinctive General Electric 'Turtleback' combined distributor magneto. As the mud was cleared one of these units was uncovered still in place and clearly bearing its 'GEC' logo cast into the casing. This engine was therefore from 43-22336 flown by 2nd Lt. Norman Zuber. Perhaps this was the propeller that was seen protruding from a ball of flame as it fell to earth 60 years before.

'Day 2' Saw the opening of what was to be one of the biggest ever trenches on TimeTeam. Geophys had already produced a remarkably aeroplane shaped printout after passing their instruments over the site of 43-22298 (Hubbard's plane) - complete with wings - much to the amusement of an incredulous Tony Robinson. It came as no surprise to the members of Lancashire Aircraft Investigation Team. Crash photos and aerial surveys had shown what lay below, but what condition it would be in after 60 years no one could predict.

As the cockpit area began to emerge things appeared promising. Solid looking skinning covered the fuselage sides and wing roots, but then it was realised that this was the thick duralumin cladding fitted as extra protection against small arms fire when attacking ground targets at low level. As the wings and remains of the rear fuselage emerged it became clear that the airframe had become a 20th Century 'fossil' with much of the metal being replaced by crystalline corrosion products and concreted mud. The distinctive outline of a Douglas Invader made an impressive sight. Conditions were sticky to say the least as the final layer of mud was cleared from the fuselage by hand to avoid damage. Sinking deep into the glutinous morass was a constant problem, but TimeTeam supervisor Kerry Ely found a nice solid object to stand on and save him from losing his wellies; his handy foothold was a .50 calibre Browning machine gun! This was the EOD team's cue to emerge from their tent and, with the film crew in position, the gun was removed to their custody to be X-rayed to ensure no live ammunition was present.

As the digging progressed the layer of hard sand that formed the original surface that the aircraft had landed on 60 years before was reached. The uncovered fuselage was now seen to be only some three to four feet high - it had fallen flat with almost no forward momentum. The sides of the fuselage had ballooned out as if it had been squashed flat. The gunner's control position in the rear fuselage had completely collapsed, no longer having the structure of the severed tail unit to support it. The sides had burst outwards and the glazed escape hatch, once set in the top of the fuselage, was found lying on the sand, pinned down by a large and heavy cylindrical object that had fallen from the upper section of the rear bomb bay.

Above: The wings of Hubbard's A-26 emerge from the mud.

Opposite page top: Although impressive, it was discovered that the tail of Hubbard's plane had become a modern-day 'fossil' held together by mud and corrosion.

The perforated cooling sleeves of the twin .50 Brownings protruding from the domed cover quickly identified this as the remotely operated upper gun turret, part of one of the most sophisticated airborne fire control systems of WW2. Back at the tail section, the trench was by now taking on the appearance of a small lagoon, with the now fully exposed rear fuselage still clearly marked with its 'Star & Bar' insignia. Unfortunately hopes of lifting the fuselage in one piece were diminishing rapidly, with a serious crack from the impact now opening up, coupled with a large section of the underside having been torn out when the lower turret fell away as the plane broke up in the air. The turret itself was found in a tidal gutter between the two sites.

As the third day of filming dawned it became clear that it would not be possible to excavate a complete aircraft. The tail section had yet to be lifted, an operation planned for Day 1. Digging and mud clearing operations struggled on regardless. The full length of the starboard wing and the shattered spars protruding from the torn-off port wing were exposed. Beyond the rear fuselage a further section of airframe came to light. This was the starboard engine nacelle that had been swept from the wing by the force of the impact. Priority was given to clearing the cockpit

The .50 Browning machine gun that stopped Kerry sinking into the mud.

and centre fuselage, the latter proving almost impossible due to the burnt and shredded remains of the centre self-sealing fuel tank.

The cockpit showed signs of a brief, but intense, fire with charred wiring but no signs of any instrumentation or flying controls. Also absent was the complicated hydraulic system. It was concluded that although the wreck had not been recovered, there had been a thorough and systematic stripping out of most of the avionics - hardly surprising as the A-26 was probably the technical equivalent in its day of the Eurofighters that constantly over-flew the site. The pilots flew so low it was obvious that they were trying to get a look at the dig! The cockpit revealed dramatic evidence of the impact as the folded nose wheel assembly, complete with intact wheel and tyre, had been forced up through the cockpit floor.

With the lift of the tail finally completed, diggers were freed to finish the excavation. The upper turret was lifted in one piece, though largely held together with mud, and the starboard engine was cleared ready to lift.

AFTER DAY THREE

Although filming had finished on day three, the excavation team was given permission to use the equipment for a fourth day. It was decided to excavate the second aircraft that had been totally destroyed in the crash and subsequent fire, as any further disturbance of Hubbard's aircraft would have simply resulted in its total disintegration. Progress was rapid and as the mud was scooped away it was clear that Zuber's aircraft had broken up in the crash. The wings had been reduced to little more than a pair of girder-like spars, the upper gun turret was badly corroded

and rapidly disintegrated. The tail was completely missing and the cockpit badly smashed. Only the cockpit floor remained because it had been embedded in the sand and had escaped the fire. The complete nose wheel assembly was still folded into its well underneath. Other smaller finds included the control column, the pilot's seat and - the pilot's ashtray! Strange to think that the pilot, surrounded by hundreds of gallons of high-octane fuel, was allowed to smoke.

The items found in this second excavation were recorded and a sketch showed that Zuber's aircraft had come to rest, broken in half, with the tail at 90 degrees to the forward fuselage; again indicating a weak point around the gunner's position. It was also apparent that the two aircraft had come to rest nose to nose. This, together with the scatter of the remaining engines, gave the distinct impression that the two planes had spiralled down, out-of control, following the collision. Sadly the collision took place too low for anyone to have a chance of baling out.

THE INVESTIGATION

With so much new information available the assembled experts were able to re-examine the circumstances surrounding the crash. It had been assumed that this was a simple take-off accident when one aircraft had flown into the back of the other, but the evidence suggested otherwise. The A-26 Invader had only come into operational use shortly before the accident, but a major problem had already emerged; pilots were having difficulty seeing beyond the prominent engine nacelles. A revised canopy had quickly been drawn up to at least partly alleviate the problem, but revising the production line and modifying aircraft already delivered was giving Douglas further headaches. Hubbard's aircraft appeared from the records to have been fitted with the original style of canopy and this was confirmed during the excavation. Zuber's, on the other hand, should have had a revised canopy, perhaps

The engine and propeller from Zuber's plane.

this why Hubbard was accompanied by a flight engineer and Zuber was not? In the event it made no difference. A large gouge in the top of the tail section appeared to indicate that the first contact had been made in this area. A propeller had then sliced into the top of the gunner's compartment and damaged this, weaker, glazed section of the airframe. The weight of the ventral turret behind this position then led to the break-up of the fuselage. Though no distinctive propeller slashes were found in the airframe sections, collision damage was clearly visible on the propeller blades of both aircraft. The evidence seemed to point to the two aircraft having almost become locked together - especially as the two wrecks came down within 80 feet of each other.

In the final analysis there seems little point in trying to attribute blame for this incident. The most important outcome of the project was the opportunity to uncover and properly record one of the most intact aircraft wrecks in the UK, whilst there was still enough left to examine. The advanced state of corrosion was a great surprise. Even the virtually anaerobic conditions of the marsh could not prevent the aircraft alloys disintegrating, providing a graphic warning that wreckage at all such crash sites will eventually corrode away.

ACKNOWLEDGEMENTS

Andy Saunders	Jean-Pierre Ducellier	Gareth Jones
Neil Faulkner	Alan Brown	Ian Hutton
Nadia Durrani	Edwina Silver	Julian Evan-Hart
Steve Vizard	Peter Arnold	Ian Hodgkiss
John Foreman	Chris Bennett	Ian McLachlan
James Cutler	Jeff Carless	Leo Lyon
Cy Chadwick	Peter Cornwell	Mark Kirby
Alex Bateman	Philippa Wheeler	Brian Fernley
Sue Raftree	Martine Gourlain	Nick Wotherspoon
Pierre Ben	Guy de la Bédoyère	Michael C Fox

BIBLIOGRAPHY

'Aces High' by Shores and Williams, published by Grub Street in 1994.
'Bader's Last Fight' by Andy Saunders, published by Grub Street in 2007.
'Battle of Britain - then and now' editor Winston Ramsey, published by After the Battle in 1980.
'Battle of France - then and now' by Peter Cornwell, published by After the Battle in 2007.
'Dambusters - the definitive history' by Ward, Lee and Wachtel, published by Red Kite in 2003.
'Eighth Air Force Bomber Stories' by Ian McLachlan, published by Sutton in 2004.
'Final Flights' by Ian McLachlan, published by PSL in 1989.
'In Search of the Zeppelin War – The Archaeology of the First Blitz' by Dr Neil Faulkner
 and Dr Nadia Durrani, published by Grub Street in 2007.
'Knights of the Skies' by Michael C Fox, published by Air Research in 2006.
'TimeTeam Companion' by Tim Taylor, published by Channel 4 Books in 1999.
'Zeppelin' by Ray Rimell, published by Conway in 1984.
'Zeppelin over Suffolk' by Mark Mower, published by Pen and Sword in 2008.